D1609219

BODY IN QUESTION

JEROME SILBERGELD

P.Y. and Kinmay W. Tang Center for East Asian Art
Department of Art and Archaeology, Princeton University
in association with Princeton University Press

BODY IN QUESTION

Image and Illusion in Two Chinese Films by Director Jiang Wen

Titles in the Tang Center Lecture Series are listed at the end of this volume.

Published by the P.Y. and Kinmay W. Tang Center for East Asian Art
Department of Art and Archaeology, Princeton University, Princeton, New Jersey 08544-1018
in association with Princeton University Press

Distributed by Princeton University Press, 41 William Street, Princeton, New Jersey 08540-5237
press.princeton.edu

Copyright © 2008 by the Trustees of Princeton University
In the Nation's Service and in the Service of All Nations
All Rights Reserved

Library of Congress Control Number: 2008927584
ISBN: 978-0-691-13946-3

British Library Cataloging-in-Publication Data is available

Managing Editor: Dora C.Y. Ching
Copy Editor: Joseph N. Newland
Design, composition, and production: Binocular, New York

This book was typeset in DIN.
Printed in Singapore

10 9 8 7 6 5 4 3 2 1

Cover illustration: Film frame from *In the Heat of the Sun*, directed by Jiang Wen, 1994

CONTENTS

Acknowledgments

Jiang Wen, speaking recently of his new (third) film, *Taiyang zhaocheng shengqi*, *The Sun Also Rises*, said, "I cannot tell you just what this film is all about. If I was able to express it clearly in speech, I wouldn't have made the film." The filmmaker's work is done, and until my own work was done I did not ask Jiang Wen whether my own interpretation of these two films, *In the Heat of the Sun* and *Devils on the Doorstep*, makes good sense to him or not. This is the author's problem, and for readers to judge. But I want to express my deep gratitude to Jiang Wen for so readily answering the few specific questions that I simply could not resist asking along the way and for his invaluable discussion with me afterwards.

In preparing this book, I was given many opportunities to present parts of it in guest lectures that provided encouragement and valuable feedback. For this, I am grateful to Karen Hwang and Eugene Wang at Harvard; Wu Hung at the University of Chicago; Michael Knight at the San Francisco Asian Art Museum; Greg Olsen at the Seattle Art Museum; Hui-shu Lee and Lothar von Falkenhausen at UCLA; Louise Edwards at the Australian National University and the University of Technology, Sydney; Martin Powers at the University of Michigan; Robert Harrist at Columbia University; Yve-Alain Bois of the Institute for Advanced Study, Princeton; Tang Center for East Asian Art, Princeton University; and Jiayan Mi of The College of New Jersey.

I am especially grateful to Yingjin Zhang, University of California at San Diego, and Jason McGrath at the University of Minnesota for their thorough reading of my manuscript and their many thoughtful suggestions.

Joseph Newland, as text editor, attended to every detail, offered numerous corrections and suggestions, and put up with far too many of my "final" and "absolutely final" alterations. Book designers Joseph Cho and Stefanie Lew of Binocular, combined good taste and remarkable creativity. To the three of them, my lasting gratitude.

My daughter, Emily Silbergeld, did most of the indexing for this volume, not to mention offering bits and pieces of unasked-for but valuable criticism along the way.

Lance Herrington, at Princeton University's New Media Center, worked many little miracles in helping to make the DVD that accompanies this volume.

For various kinds of assistance big and small, I am grateful to Liu Dan, Gong Jisui, and Jiang Wen's assistant Yin Hongbo in Beijing; at Princeton to Kim Wishart for her editorial assistance, Kyle Steinke, Jun Hu, and Fan Jiang.

For their major assistance at Princeton, I would like to thank the Tang family and the Tang Center for East Asian Art.

Dora Ching, associate director of the Tang Center for East Asian Art at Princeton, has helped in more ways than I can count.

Every one of my books, including several intended to be my "last," has been dedicated to my family — Michelle, David, Emily — because they are the ones who sustain me.

INTRODUCTION: BODY TALK

Jiang Wen, star actor in such films as *Hibiscus Town* and *Red Sorghum*, has written and directed his own screenplays for two films, *In the Heat of the Sun* (1994) and *Devils on the Doorste*p (2000). The former was China's box-office leader in its first year and swept Taiwan's 1996 Golden Horse awards, including best film of the year, best direction (Jiang Wen[1]), best original screenplay (Jiang Wen), best cinematography (Gu Changwei[2]), best actor (Xia Yu[3]), and best sound recording (Gu Changning, the cinematographer's brother[4]). Despite this popularity, *In the Heat of the Sun* remains virtually unseen in America and has become virtually unavailable here in both film and DVD formats, as if banned in accordance with some kind of afterthought. The latter film, *Devils on the Doorstep*, won the Jury Grand Prix at Cannes in 2000, subsequent to which the film was banned from distribution and Jiang Wen was banned personally from film directing in China for an indefinite period (which turned out to be five years).[5] The film has never been approved for distribution in China and has not been distributed commercially in Western theaters; it was belatedly released on Japanese DVD in 2002 and American DVD in 2005.

What leads me to write about these two films is threefold: that they are good (so aesthetically well-crafted), that they are interesting (even if they weren't so "good," they are so stimulating), and that they have so much more than first meets the eye (they reward the task of repeated viewing and encourage the writer's intermediation, turning viewers into readers). As an occasional teacher of Chinese cinema (more regularly of Chinese painting history) whose demanding standards for "class-worthy" new films are satisfied only once every few years, I found Jiang Wen's two films irresistible and I hope other writers will also, for there is surely much more to be said about them than I have set down here.

Film scholar Jason McGrath, in serving as one of my readers, commented: "No source that I'm aware of has so far read the two films together, even though they were made by the same director/cinematographer team…probably because the films are very different in both cinematic style and narrative content." At first sight, these two films seem almost to have come from different directors, from a different team of filmmakers. Although both are set in the past (unlike most recent Chinese films, which have eschewed this historical mode as old-fashioned "Fifth Generation" stuff[6]), one takes place in the pre-Revolutionary era, one in the Cultural Revolution; one is set among rural peasants, the other is set among an urban elite; one is filmed primarily in black-and-white and one primarily in color; one is cynical and dismissive, one is totally sincere and truly passionate. There are other similarities as well, less obvious perhaps: both combine an exceptional sense of humor with an experience in full measure of loss, tragedy, and even horror; the color film concludes in black-and-white and *vice-versa*; both are the work of dedicated filmmakers (director, cinematographer, and film editors) whose attentiveness to the finest level of detail can hardly even be seen by a movie house audience and seems to be there mostly to satisfy their own sense of perfected artistry. And yet, what draws them together more than similarity is complementarity. Together, as we will see in the end, they complete an agenda.

There is much to look for in a film, and I have chosen one thing to focus on, put simply: body talk. The concept of "embodiment" embodies a range of allegorical and ironic possibilities, from the theoretical to the purely literal. In providing concrete form to the metaphoric process, anything from an inanimate building to a fashionable hat to the particularized details of a human face or body will do. A recent edited volume on the subject includes scholarly studies of "bodily" forms ranging from Buddhist relics to painted flowers, from calligraphic traces to ghosts, embodying all things from "the flow of *qi*" to sexual desire, and from imperial authority to the "spirit of a passing age."[7] Much of contemporary artist Gu Wenda's work is based on transformations of body parts, disembodied and re-embodied in artistic form — for example, human hair gathered from all around the world, woven into words and characters (*United Nations Series*, 1993 onward), or powdered, boiled, and molded into "biological ink sticks" (*Ink Alchemy*, 1999–2001), the basic elements and media of literature, writing and painting, made literally from the people who use them. This comes with an ironic twist: the ink is not made for use, the words and characters are unreadable.

However, what we might see as metaphor, allegory, and analogy, many or most in China might see as a form of real identity, not of two things merely juxtaposed and similar by way of coincidence but as a shared, if varied, identity of things by virtue of deriving from a common set of generative principles. A coherent system of principles, for example, closely relates the Chinese practices of traditional medicine, which features the body as earth, and of architectural siting or *fengshui,* in which one sees the metaphoric earth-as-body.[8] Thus, a recent article by Cary Liu describes how

> Architecture can then be seen as manifesting imperishable words and potent patterns — *embodied images*. In architecture, embodiment can take the form of numerology, geomancy, cosmology, building rites and deities, sumptuary regulations, and symbology.

To this list of things embodied in architectural form one might add, among others: regional identity and local pride; the present and future health and well-being of a resident family (or the lack of it); and in a word, taste (or in two words, which remind us just how much a word or two *won't* do, "bad" taste). Liu continues,

> … but it is also important to take into consideration the way embodied words and patterns are transmitted. With the distance of geography or the passage of time, new meanings are often superimposed, dressed in new forms, functions, and materials.[9]

In other words, the embodiment of something in concrete form does not mean that the meaning of the embodiment is fixed, for the significance of embodied forms fluctuates with authorial intent and audience interpretation.

In this volume, "body talk" means both the body doing the equivalent of talking (significant postures, gestures, stances, actions) and, conversely, talk about bodies. Bodies "talking" involves both acculturated and universal languages, and most images embody both. Liu Jun's 1985 photograph (fig. 1) is a classic of both composition and content, and its body talk is the basis of both. Among my students, those from China are quicker than their American counterparts to judge, from his clothing and his aloof pose, that the tall standing figure is the local Party leader, the village cadre, caught up in a minidrama that illustrates his alienation from the masses he is supposed to serve. The single-frame photograph lacks the information provided by an ongoing cinematic narrative: namely, that the horizontal counterpart to this towering figure, his intense emotion the counterpart to the standing figure's aloofness, is the victim of the cadre's physical assault. But once this information is shared, the body language is no longer a local dialect but one that can be read by all. The look on the victim's face tells the story: prevented by status from defending himself, though he may be suffering from a punch to the stomach or a kick to the crotch, the open-mouthed expression of agony is no more one of physical pain than it is of boundless frustration. How much humiliation can one—must one—endure? His eyes squeezed tightly shut, he is beyond sympathy and comfort. Yet two villagers, one older, one young, attend to the victim's physical distress. Focusing their attention downward, the villagers' sympathies are evident. None dares to look at the cadre, just as he looks at none of them. Their disgust, their disdain, is manifest without words. Do they also fear him? What is it that maintains his singular authority and restrains the hostility of all those who surround him? Folding his arms and refusing visual contact, is he really as confident as this invincible pose suggests, or does his arrogant posture mask some insecurity beneath? What, one wonders, is the future of this relationship between the masses and the people? The theme of the photograph and the language that it uses are those of *In the Heat of the Sun*.[10]

Figure 1 Liu Jun, *The Village Cadre Knocking the Old Villager Down to the Ground*, black-and-white photograph, 1985. Guangdong Museum of Art. From Wang Huangsheng and Hu Wugong, eds., *Zhongguo renben, jishi zai dangdai: Humanism in China, A Contemporary Record of Photography*, 195.

The substitution of body image for verbal communication is especially important in a film culture "where the censorship of film scripts in their textual formulation shifts the filmmakers' primary negotiable space to the realm of unspoken images, a richly encoded visual realm where textual pursuit alone may falter but where the art historian travels most comfortably."[11] This includes the metaphoric substitution of individual bodies for something larger than themselves, ideas or institutions, which is the basis of the interpretation of *In the Heat of the Sun* set forth in this volume, as well as the human body–animal body exchange, both anthropomorphism and zoomorphism, so important in *Devils on the Doorstep*.[12] Body talk places an emphasis on film as a visual art form. Talk about bodies, on the other hand, exhibits a marked lack of fixity. Time and again in these films, one can watch closely as the same body, unchanged, evokes remarkably diverse or rapidly changing perceptions, less responsive to the body itself than to the inner, psychological world of the respondent.[13] This depends surprisingly little on cinematographic image. On the other hand, as we will see, the filmmakers themselves can do the "talking," in a purely visual way, through the knowing juxtaposition of people and animal counterparts in telling situations. It is within this responsive fluidity that these two films' bodily discourse takes place, highlighting the twin pairings of nostalgia/misremembrance and fraternization/bestialization.

Advancing theory is not the aim of this book. But for a culture like China's, in which, what we (from a somewhat different perspective than theirs) call "allegory" and the "analogical mode" reign supreme in rhetorical expression as the circumspect means of negotiating with censorship, a careful bit of body watching — the figure taken figuratively — can be a very useful tool in trying to understand the unstated or understated. The careful observation of form can take one beyond the obvious in textual narrative, to a level in which the significance of the narrative, made subtle for the sake of both artistry and political subversion, is itself embodied. This observational process is essentially the same for all art-historical disciplines, whether traditional or modern, two-dimensional or three-, static or kinetic. ∎

BODY VISIBLE

In the Heat of the Sun

In the Heat of the Sun (*Yangguang canlan de rizi*) **DIRECTOR:** Jiang Wen **SCREENPLAY:** Jiang Wen
ORIGINAL TEXT: Wang Shuo, novella *Dongwu xiongmeng* (*Wild Beasts*) **CINEMATOGRAPHY:** Gu
Changwei **FILM EDITING:** Zhou Ying **MUSIC:** Guo Wenjing **DESIGN:** Chen Haozheng, Li Yongxin
PRODUCERS: Manfred Wong, Liu Xiaoqing, Guo Youliang, Hsu An-chin, Ki Po **PRODUCTION STUDIOS**
Hong Kong Dragon Film, China Film Co-Production Studio, Lou Yi Ltd., Studio Bobelsberg
CAST: Xia Yu (Ma Xiaojun), Han Dong (Ma Xiaojun, child), Jiang Wen (Ma Xiaojun, adult), Ning
ing (Mi Lan), Geng Le (Liu Yiku), Liu Xiaoning (Liu Yiku, adult), Tao Hong (Yu Beipei), Wang
Xueqi (Ma Wenzhong, Ma Xiaojun's father), Siqin Gaowa (Zhai Ru, Ma Xiaojun's mother), Feng
Xiaogang (Teacher Hu), Wang Hai (Big Ant), Shang Nan (Liu Sitian), Dai Shaopo (Yang Gao
Wang Shuo (gang leader) **Color and black-and-white, 119 minutes, 1994**

[001]

Wang Shuo

Love fused my image and your spirit's fire;
Not me you followed, but your own desire.
Pierre Corneille, *L'Illusion Comique*[14]

You see him as a saint. I'm much less awed;
In fact, I see right through him. He's a fraud.
Molière, *Tartuffe*[15]

The film script for *In the Heat of the Sun* was radically adapted and autobiographically transformed by director Jiang Wen from a novella by China's well-known bad-boy author Wang Shuo[16] [001], who shares the film-writing credits and makes his own brief appearance in the film.[17] There are many films that tell the story of this generation of filmmakers in their own youth, typically well-educated urban children "sent down" to factories or the countryside during the Cultural Revolution for re-education by workers and peasants, often in remote, minority-populated regions: *Sacrificed Youth* (1985), *Army Nurse* (1985), and *King of the Children* (1987) exemplify the genre.[18] *In the Heat of the Sun* is unique in telling the story of those sons and daughters of parents politically so well positioned at the time as to have been spared this forced rustication. Instead, these children of privilege (*gaogan zi di,* like Jiang Wen and Wang Shuo, sons of ranking military officials),[19] are abandoned to an ironic coming-of-age experience back home, in Beijing, mostly in the absence of parental guidance and clear rules of authority, while Mao Zedong's revolutionary experiment, its rhetoric of political correctness, and his politics of social upheaval, are all relegated to the distant background. In the title of his novella, Wang Shuo calls them beasts: *Dongwu xiongmeng, Wild Beasts.*

Those who have never previously heard about such children left behind, who didn't know that Mao Zedong's radical police state left much room for mindless shenanigans during that dreadful decade, might well wonder whether there is any truth at all in this film. The fact is, the narrator, who relates this tale in voice-over[20] as an uninterrupted but profoundly corrupted flashback, is an inveterate liar. And yet, while the cinematic telling proves false, the circumstances described here were real and the corruption of memory is itself not fiction but fact.[21] Yingjin Zhang refers to this film as "nostalgia for the Cultural Revolution,"[22] and that seems to be the consensus view, borne out by Jiang Wen's own statement, "For people my age, the Cultural Revolution was actually a lot of fun. We were just kids being kids."[23] But it is hardly that simple. Not only was Jiang Wen, born in 1963 to a senior captain in the People's Liberation Army (PLA), only three years old at the outbreak of the Cultural Revolution, but *Heat of the Sun's* critique goes far beyond nostalgia and "having fun," and, indeed, far beyond the confusion of time and memory, and far beyond the Cultural Revolution itself.

In the Heat of the Sun is the very definition of a subversive film. In a censorial culture which leaves no room for uncertainty in matters of politics, no ambiguous middle ground for those locked in struggle between revolution and counterrevolution, no gray area between the worlds of light and dark, the narrator's self-confessed lies subtly yet radically subvert the fundamental values of the Communist Revolution and the rhetorical devices of its propagandists. The narrator frequently mistakes his own mischief for heroics [002]. Through him, revolutionary posturing is unmasked and the heroics of the Revolution are satirized as the trivial play of spoiled children. Everyone is skewered, from the movie heroes of the day, whose most popular lines the boy quotes verbatim and unintentionally pollutes in his own childish antics, to his own father, who is mostly absent on political missions but tells him "I'm your father, I know everything." The son masquerades in his father's military uniform when daddy isn't home, but the core truth which the boy discovers hidden in the father's army journal, rather than heroic adventures, is a concealed condom [003], which he accidentally punctures then naively returns to its hiding place and so, unwittingly, involves in the production of China's next generation. By the end, the accumulation of self-aware narrative ironies and

[002]

[003]

Condom

outright falsehoods mirror a society in which the repression of thought and speech generates a paranoid public that habitually says one thing while thinking another and undermines the plausibility of *any* "truth" in general. How, then, is the film to unpack these lies and convey any truth of its own?

The film's jarring mixture of truth and untruth — small, brazen, picaresque untruths that add up to a greater and mightily unhappy truth — is matched by the mixed form of this drama: a comedy that enfolds a tragedy, a comedy (at first) that leaves nothing (in the end) to laugh about, for what it deals with is no laughing matter. As a parable, it is encapsulated on both ends by a narrator — heard as a youth at the outset, and as an adult at the conclusion — who shakes his finger at Chinese authorities to expose their foolery as no better than his own. What is undone in the process is faith. Faith in the Communist ideology. Faith in the system. And worse than just that: faith in people. For all those who once held any kind of faith in China, this is a dire tragedy.

Perhaps Chinese drama has never before so clearly and so cynically toyed with the audience's faith in what they see with their own eyes. Western theater, by contrast, has worked this device innumerable times since the time of Pierre Corneille's *L'Illusion Comique*, first produced in 1639 (fig. 2). In that play, the magician Alcandre reveals to an estranged father more than he cares to see about the scandalous life and eventual death of his son, only to reveal at the

Figure 2 Performance of Pierre Corneille's *L'Illusion Comique*, showing the magician Alcandre, National Theater of Belgium, June 1969. From Alain Niderst, ed., *Pierre Corneille: The Théâtre Complet*, tome 1, vol. 2, following 555.

end that the son's death was nothing more than part of a theatrical performance played out by the still-living son as a stage actor in Paris, an illusion much like Alcandre's own sleight-of-hand magic show.[24] Momentarily stripped of meaningful context by the magician, the audience is as much taken in and dismayed by the comedic illusion as the father is. How contrary to those informative theatrical traditions ranging from the Greek chorus to the Shakespearean aside, designed to assure that the audience got the point. Corneille's own description of its compounded form could readily be applied to Jiang Wen's film; he wrote in introducing his play:

> Here is a strange monster which I am dedicating. The first act is only a prologue, the next three constitute an imperfect comedy, the last one a tragedy, and all of this sewn together forms a comedy. Let people dub it a bizarre and extravagant invention as much as they like, it is new.[25]

Not long afterward came Molière's theater of unmasking, with his first version of *Tartuffe* premiering at Versailles in 1664. The tradition of the "unreliable narrator" thrives in modern Western literature, from Twain's Huck Finn through Nabokov's Humbert Humbert. But for China in the 1990s, Jiang Wen's film was still something new, and even today, when the laughing stops it is a human tragedy deep enough to make any thoughtful audience cry. Corneille's sleight-of-hand was a self-reflexive commentary on theater and audience; Jiang Wen's is about the illusions and self-delusions of politics.

A Western audience untutored in Chinese events and Chinese ways cannot be expected to fully recognize the parable embodied by this group of children: take, for example, an online review signed "littlesiddie" (Sidney Clark) from Cambridge, Massachusetts, reading, "The worst thing about this movie is that it didn't help me to learn anything about China, its people or its countryside. Everything was very glossy and squeaky clean, like a travel brochure, and hence cold and unengaging."[26] In his dissident dance around the censor, the Chinese filmmaker's route is necessarily indirect. As an artist, his tactics are little different from those of his Mongol-period or Manchu-era predecessors, overtly visual but cunningly allegorical, and a thoughtful use of embodiment is one of his most important means of evasion.[27] This film's first shots, for example, begin with an alternating, dialectical series of normal and abnormal images: successively, a gigantic sculpture of Chairman Mao (see frame 037), under whose singular authority and direct gaze all else (including the movie itself) takes place, followed by a mother swatting her spoiled child (whom we soon come to know as our troubled storyteller) in public — hardly a common image in Chinese family cinema; then an airplane embodying China's martial-patriotic spirit, followed by a child (the same) at a military ceremony loudly blowing his father's whistle, usurping the "voice" of authority and disrupting the event; thirdly, a group of young dancing girls whose ballet embodies their ideal love of Chairman Mao, being suggestively spied upon by our child-narrator as a gang of boys shatters the window of their dance studio. These sequenced pairs repeatedly knock the icons off of their pedestals and all-in-all suggest the out-of-control chaos of the age. These are not unambiguous symbols in the classic sense but embodied images deriving meaning from their unique contiguity within the film. At the risk of reductionism, ten exam-ples are presented here in which such embodiment encapsulates the film's narrative sequence and, more importantly, through which the film reveals its significance.

Belief and disbelief: clothes that come to life and disembodied people
As in films like Chen Kaige's *King of the Children*, Communist authority is embodied in the form of a teacher [004] — a tall, thin, humorless, petty auto-crat, a stereotype handed down from Confucian times. But by the time of this narration, teachers and intellectuals were among the most vulnerable targets and conspicuous victims of the Cultural Revolution and its assault on the established centers of authority, and those who survived were those least worthy of attack and most willing to conform to the rapidly changing demands of the day. *King of the Children*'s Lao Gar resisted living up to this "ideal" of the subordinate teacher,[28] but true to form, *Heat of the Sun*'s unsmil-ing Teacher Hu delivers to an unsmiling class [005] a lesson straight out of the book on how China justly acquired territorial authority from Russia over Manchuria (a lesson that plays straight into the children's heroic fantasies). As he does so, however, he is confronted by a minor miracle: before his eyes — our eyes — of its own accord, his hat repeatedly flies off of the desk where he has placed it [006] [007]. Allegorically, this "king of the children" is stripped of his

Teacher Hu

[004]

[005]

Classroom 1

[006]

[007]

[008]

The teacher's hat; Teacher Hu: "Don't laugh.

Coals for the teacher

clothing, subjected to cinematic ridicule that undermines his credibility and seems more like something drawn from Tom Sawyer's rowdy school days (the teacher, "always severe…seemed to take a vindictive pleasure in punishing the least shortcomings" while the students "spent their days in terror and suffering and their nights in plotting revenge"[29]) than anything one expects to find in a good socialist classroom. Refusing to acknowledge the impossibility of the matter or to accept embarrassment for what is really happening, Teacher Hu replaces the hat but stubbornly upholds the authority of scientific materialism, telling the students, "Don't laugh. It's a simple principle of physics" [008]. But of course it isn't: it's a film director's joke and Hu is the butt of it. He suspects his own innocent students, not the film director, but when he repeatedly looks around to catch them in the act of subversion, no one is moving. They sit perfectly still. This is not because a display of perfect behavior. The audience has already seen that they are all too ready to taunt and laugh behind the teacher's back; but entranced by the self-mobilized hat, they may not notice that the director has presented the equivalent of a single film frame over and over, approximately 176 times, spread over three separate "shots": a frozen image of disembodied children, a parody of the robotic obedience he demands of them and the opposite of how they really feel — like a still photograph parading as cinema [005] [009]. He perhaps has good reason to worry that the strings of his own ideological puppetry might be revealed to the students, when the impossibly mobile hat is suddenly stabilized on his desk by a pile of coal that appears out of nowhere, filling the hat beyond its brim [010]. With this contravention of natural law, all the rules of the game are suddenly suspended: the authority "naturally" vested in the teacher devolves to the unauthorized and undisciplined, to the students, and with it, allegorically, Chinese authority over Manchuria flies out of the window. The entire scene might be enjoyed as nothing more than a classroom romp, but it launches this allegory on a comic wave that later washes up as tragedy.

Body of desire and disgust

Credence and faith, displaced, seek an outlet elsewhere. That the narrator's desire initially targets a young, attractive female body is hardly surprising. Chinese film culture has long privileged the unruly male who discovered faith through a female attachment. Republican-period, Maoist, and post-Mao cinema have all regularly done this. Ma Xiaojun, the film's young deceiver, is already a master forger of keys and for thrills spends time breaking into neighborhood apartments, which poses little risk since most of their inhabitants have already been sent down to the countryside for indefinite periods; and since, like Goldilocks, he typically steals nothing more than a meal and a nap in some stranger's bed, he leaves little trace of his exploits. Xiaojun forges tales as readily he does keys, and he enters into his own tales as he does the empty apartments of others, which he fills with voyeuristic fantasy uninterrupted by reality. When Xiaojun first spies the body of Mi Lan it is from an awkward vantage point beneath her bed, where he has dived in haste when surprised by her return to the apartment he has snuck into [011]. Trapped there breathlessly as she changes her clothes and then goes out again, all he (and the camera, which has followed him there) can see of her is legs and panties. One cannot be sure of his response at this first sight of her [012], yet it is readily evident that she hasn't the legs or the rear end of a model film star but is notably thick-ankled and chunky.[30] Although handsome of face and readily able to fix Ma Xiaojun with a determined glance [013], her pudginess will first be remarked upon by Xiaojun's fellow punks, who attribute her broad bottom to sex with too many boyfriends. Xiaojun laughs this one off, but he is made aware by this remark of both her imperfection and the vulnerability of his own affections. Later on, when he has become increasingly frustrated by Mi Lan's preference for an older, more desirable member of the gang and adolescent resentment begins to turn him against her, it is her imperfect paunch that he chooses to insult ("You're certainly fat enough.... It's like you've just had a baby.") before kicking her into a swimming pool with a foot to the butt [014]. The pure object of desire becomes an imperfect object of conflicted feelings, attraction and disgust, embodying both his longing and his feelings of rejection, a woman sought after with increasing desperation yet increasingly ripe for abuse. But what does Mi Lan embody?

Under the bed

[011]

[012]

Mi Lan's legs

Mi Lan

Ideals/illusions embodied

Before actually seeing Mi Lan in the flesh, Ma Xiaojun had already become enamored of her by means of a photograph of her in a red swimsuit, hanging in her apartment — on the wall above her bed, where it becomes the object of his romantic attachment [015]. The audience will no doubt identify this with the swimsuit she wears later when he attaches his foot to her bottom, already mentioned. Red, once traditionally the color associated with celebration, sexual desire, and the ceremony of marriage, a youthful color abandoned by married women, was appropriated in modern times for the Revolution and the Party. Romantic longing is transformed into ideological ambition, embodied in the person of Chairman Mao himself — "the red, red sun in our hearts," the only legitimate love in the most radical of times. Xiaojun (literally, "Little Soldier"), the brat son of a midlevel People's Liberation Army Officer, imagines himself a loyal soldier ("I longed for a Sino-Soviet war," the narrator recalls. "I was sure that in a new world war the PLA's iron fist would smash the Soviets and Americans. A new war hero would become a legend — that's me, of course."), and an attractive, red-draped young girl is just the thing to arouse his mixed-up, hormonally-fueled patriotism. Hers is a "political body," redolent of sexual romance but also of Mao Zedong's "Revolutionary Romanticism," with its infusion of desire and fantasy into reality politics.[31] But despite the ancient and well-developed precedent for Chinese political narrative appropriating a romantic verse,[32] as in the case of Qu Yuan's fourth-century BCE *Nine Songs*, revealing the underlying sexuality of the politically appropriated body is bound to arouse consternation and resistance (as one would find surrounding academic studies of the sexuality of Jesus[33]). Any discussion of Mao, the Party, and sexual desire could be a long one, but a few exemplary notes will have to suffice.

The unusual children of this film scarcely resemble any of those seen before in film, popularized in memoirs, or encountered in most academic case studies[34] of the period. Whereas most youngsters his age would have lodged their fantasies in the political posters that proliferated throughout the nation, the dominant visual icons of their day, Ma Xiaojun's narrative turns on his entrancement by a personal photograph, intimate and fetching (hanging, strangely enough, where one might expect instead to see Chairman Mao

[015]

Photograph: the girl-in-red

enshrined). Still, many of those posters offered a substantial dose of sexual sublimation, as Xiaomei Chen describes in remembrance of her own youthful viewing. Describing the 1970 poster *Full of Hatred* (*Manqiang chouhen*) (fig. 3), from a scene in the ballet *Red Detachment of Women*, she writes,

> Wu Qinghua is in chains, tortured by the oppressive landlord who imprisoned her to prevent her escape. For Western audiences, her handcuffed hands, whipped body, long and braided hair, and torn red silk dress not unlike that of the teasing Victoria's Secret lingerie might invite sexual and perhaps even masochistic fantasy with or without any knowledge of China. For audiences within China in that period, however, the embodiment of youth, beauty, grace, passion, and energy that the model theater heroines featured on posters and other artworks was one of the rare decorations to be seen in public spaces and private homes, and as such the models could be gazed on with the same intensity as pictures of Marilyn Monroe, whose seductiveness had magnetized both the powerful few and the common people. Today, looking back, I am aware that my treasuring of these images was not unrelated to their voluptuous appeal and bodily beauty, which was securely disguised by the focus on an ideologically correct story and by equipping the womanly body with a "manly spirit," as it was traditionally defined.[35]

The youthful confusion of orgiastic politics and sex experienced by Ma Xiaojun in viewing this photograph and pursuing its subject was shared by director

Figure 3 Unknown artist, *Full of Hatred* (*Manqiang chouhen*), poster based on oil painting, 1970. Library of Congress. From Harriet Evans and Stephanie Donald, eds., *Picturing Power in the People's Republic of China*, 111.

Figure 4 Unknown artist from the Shanghai People's Publishing House, *Modern and Revolutionary Dance: Red Detachment of Women*, poster based on filmed ballet, 1971. From Stewart Fraser, ed., *100 Great Chinese Posters: Recent Examples of the "People's Art" from the People's Republic of China*, pl. 25.

Jiang Wen (also called Xiaojun in his childhood), who recalls nostalgically his own early viewing of *The Red Detachment of Women* (fig. 4; Xie Jin's 1961 film, translated at Premier Zhou Enlai's suggestion into a model ballet in 1964, refilmed in 1970, and seen briefly in *Heat of the Sun*): "Watching the women on the stage with guns and short shorts, that was the first time I ever experienced sexual feelings."[36]

The identification of sex with politics — young Mi Lan in her red swimsuit with the old lion, Chairman Mao, body with body politic — lies at the core of this coming-of-age film, with its rich mixture of sincere and false hopes, hormonally charged passion and first disappointment. Late in the film, Mi Lan gives Xiaojun a birthday present, red swim shorts, to the exclamation of one of the gang members present that "She looks after you like the Party itself." Yet for a Western audience, this identification is a considerable stretch — a link absent in most film criticism and one that demands, therefore, some cultural rationalization.[37] The famous and outspoken actress Liu Xiaoqing, formerly Jiang Wen's girlfriend and his costar in *Hibiscus Town* (fig. 5), has written,

> Everyone says that you never forget your first love. I cannot really say that I ever had a first love, for in my childhood and youth the man I loved and admired most of all was Mao Zedong. I gave him everything I had: my purest love, as

well as all my longing and hopes. He was an idol I worshipped with all my heart. Chairman Mao, you were my first object of desire!… When I grew a bit older and learned the secret of how men and women made babies, I had the most shocking realization: "Could Chairman Mao possibly do *that* as well?"[38]

The answer to this embarrassed question is that even into his very late years, Mao Zedong *was* an extraordinary womanizer, a behavior he justified in traditional Daoist rather than revolutionary terms, but which was surely fueled by ordinary lust as well as by a lack of personal restraint that grew in proportion to his swelling authority (fig. 6). While effectively censored in Mao's lifetime, word of the Chairman's sexual habits gradually seeped out. Mao's physician, Li Zhisui, revealed in writing after Mao's death that the chairman had sleeping arrangements with dozens of carefully screened young women, often in multiples, and not a few boys, in the old palace, on his train, in his special chambers in the Great Hall of the People, and in bedrooms throughout the land, where he infected many of them with his venereal disease. Dr. Li wrote in the early 1990s of those sexually diseased girls whom he had to treat afterwards, "The young women were proud to be infected. The illness, transmitted by Mao, was a badge of honor, testimony to their close relations with the Chairman."[39]

The artistic sexualization of Mao, if uncommon, and outrageous to some, is not entirely new with *Heat of the Sun*. In the early 1990s, following the Tiananmen conflict in Beijing and elsewhere and the reformer Deng Xiaoping's apparent loss of moral direction, China was afflicted with something called *Mao re*, translated as "Mao Fever" or "the Mao Craze." The participants in this second, posthumous bout of Maoification shared the vision that Mao's leadership, if somewhat overheated at times, had at least provided China with a common sense of purpose and a shared sense of national pride. Figures of the late Chairman suddenly appeared everywhere, displayed on the dashboard or hanging from the rearview mirror of every taxi, on matchbooks and cigarette lighters, on wristwatches. Old Cultural Revolution buttons were dusted off and worn on new Western-style suits and exhibited in store windows everywhere. Even countercultural pop musicians like Cui Jian transformed anthems of the Revolution and the Cultural Revolution in their latest rock 'n' roll ballads, much to the government's dismay. While politically unassailable, this fashion-able Maoist nostalgia bespoke an unspeakable dissatisfaction with the cur-rent leadership, and the opportunity to define Mao slipped from the hands of official Party historians into the hands of the populace.

At this time, the avant-garde artist Li Shan entered the scene with a series of politically incorrect works (fig. 7). Technically, the realistic style of portrai-ture is orthodox. As with many of his peers, the artist's training in a state-run academy rather than being rejected is flaunted, even exaggerated, to satirical effect. Li Shan's paintings, such as that of Chairman Mao with reddened lips and a lotus flower in his mouth, produced in multiple versions by means of different color combinations, and his shift in media from oil paints to acrylics and silkscreens, unmistakably reference the most pop of all pop artists, Andy Warhol.[40] Like many of Warhol's re-reproduced pop art burlesques (fig. 8),

Figure 5 Actress Liu Xiaoqing, film frame from *Hibiscus Town*, director Xie Jin, 1986.

Figure 6 Unknown photographer, Mao Zedong meeting with student delegates to the Ninth Congress of the Communist Youth League, black-and-white photograph, 1964. From Stuart Schram, *Mao Tse-tung*, following 64.

Figure 7 (top) Li Shan, *The Rouge Series: No. 8*, silkscreen and acrylic on canvas, 1990. From Gao Minglu, ed., *Inside Out: New Chinese Art*, pl. 37. Figure 8 (left) Andy Warhol, *Mao*, silkscreen print, 1972. Vancouver Art Gallery. From Ian Thom, *Andy Warhol Images*, 86. Figure 9 (right) Edgar Snow, Mao Zedong in Baoan, Shaanxi province, black-and-white photograph, 1936 (frequently shown hand-colored). "Original" photograph reportedly in the Museum of History, Beijing. From *China Reconstructs*, November/December 1976, 27.

Figure 10 (top) Unknown photographer, Mao Zedong and acting troupe. From *China Pictorial*, November 1976, 49. **Figure 11** (left) Bodhisattva, 1038. Lower Huayan Temple, Datong, Shanxi province. From *Shanxi Yungang shiku wenwu baoguan suobian, Huayan si*, 45 **Figure 12** (right) Unknown photographer, Mao Zedong, official Communist Party I.D. photograph, mid-1930s (?), *New York Times* archival photograph.

Li Shan's Mao "portrait" is closely based on a celebrity photograph — this one from Mao's Baoan days, just before settling in at Yan'an, taken in 1936 by journalist Edgar Snow and widely reproduced ever after (often hand-colored) (fig. 9). Most striking for a Western audience, this famous photo had already been considerably touched up in early times by the state propagandists — reddened lips, plucked and thickened eyebrows, and extended "phoenix" eyes like those of ancient mythic heroes — right down to the uniform, so that the difference between touched in the photo and retouched in the painting is not as great as one might imagine.[41] In Li's painting, take away the flower and there is little difference from the photograph: a thinner, longer eyebrow, darker lips, a slightly more salacious look perhaps, but nothing more. It is not that Li has suddenly sexualized the Chairman; rather, his slight exaggerations raise the question of why was Mao so sexualized in the first place, by his own photo team? Did this merely follow some convention from the Chinese theater, where the artist Li Shan was originally trained, where dandily made-up young actors (e.g., fig. 10; note, especially, the eyes) were simultaneously heroic and feminized? Was it intended that Mao, like some Daoist immortal, should rise hermaphroditically above gender or, sexualized, like the lotus-bearing Guanyin or other attendant bodhisattvas (fig. 11), that he should seduce his following in order, ultimately, to convert and liberate them?[42] Or was it simply designed to arouse desire for the then-young Chairman, at the very the outset of his public celebrity? A look at the tired Mao on his official Party I.D. photograph at that time (fig. 12) leads one to wonder which of his early publicity photos were *not* doctored.[43]

Whereas Warhol was engaged in raising popular icons to the marketable level of "high art," Li Shan was involved in reducing a veritable icon to a level of fashionable popularity, a parody not just of Mao but even more so of the posthumous resurrection of "Mao fever" in the early 1990s, at virtually the same time as *Heat of the Sun* was being written and then filmed. For by then, Mao's sexuality was no longer secret nor a disgrace but for some the veritable mark of deification. In the post-Tiananmen era of cynicism and fallen titans, if Mao was a tyrant, if he trashed his own political subordinates, if he hit on and debauched his own women, that only showed how much more like a god he was than the earthbound leaders of more recent times. The worse he was, the better.[44] A parallel can be drawn from Robert Graves's fictional but persuasive account of Roman emperor Caligula and the hypnotic effect he had on the Germans (contrasted with the thoughtful but otherwise pathetic Claudius):

> And if he dressed as a woman; or galloped suddenly away from his army on the march; or made [his fourth wife] Caesonia appear naked before them and boasted of her beauty … this inexplicable sort of behaviour only made him the more worthy of their worship as a divine being. They used to nod wisely to each other and say, "Yes, the Gods are like that. You can't tell what they are going to do next."[45]

The emphasis in Li Shan's painting is actually less on Mao himself and more on Mao's admirers, less on their adoration of Mao during the final decade of his life, the only true love authorized and acknowledged for Chinese men and women alike, and more a disturbed commentary on the widespread revival of the Maoist cult in the early 1990s. Li's flowering of Mao is a deflowering, depriving him of any lingering pretense to innocence. And of course the Mao deflowered here is not the real Mao but the myth of Mao, not the remote and rapacious leader but the familiar and user-friendly icon, mounted on the dashboard of your local taxi.[46]

This departure from our cinematic narrative is intended to make Mi Lan's politicization more plausible and Ma Xiaojun's confusion less exceptional. His adolescent disorientation merely stands for that of an entire era, regardless of generation. In Wang Shuo's novelized version, Xiaojun asserts about the photograph of Mi Lan that "this was the first time in my life I saw a color photograph of such realistic effect, other than those of the Great Leader Chairman Mao and his close comrades-in-arms."[47] Ironically, to return to the narrative, as Xiaojun manages to secure Mi Lan's friendship and first gains legitimate entry into her apartment, she shows him her photograph [016]. Yet this picture is not hung on the wall, which is bare, but tucked away in a scrapbook. And she is not wearing a red swimsuit at all but a plain white blouse, modest and unsmiling in what turns out to be a black-and-white photo, entirely chaste in comparison to the colorful, alluring photo he remembered. This is not the ideal — not the girl, nor the Party — that he thought it was. He is confused, and

Photograph: Mi Lan in black-and-white

for the first time the audience may well be too, for it too has previously seen the color photo.

It is not as if the audience hasn't been warned. In voice-over and on-screen text, while the opening credits are still rolling against a blackened screen, the narrator confesses that "nothing is as I remember it. Change has wiped out my memories. I can't tell what's imagined from what is real." But while the audience has seen many images that deceive, in real life as in film, it is hardly used to voluntary admissions of the lie. So the images that follow pose with a matter-of-fact reality, taking priority when they contradict the text — until one image begins to contradict another. Then and only then, the audience knows: trust nobody, believe nothing, not even your own eyes. James Agee has written that "most movies are made in the evident assumption that the audience is passive and wants to remain passive; every effort is made to do all the work — the seeing, the explaining, the understanding, even the feeling."[48] *In the Heat of the Sun* not only challenges the viewer to participate, it threatens to deceive and misguide them if they do not.

Manufacturing memory through image; A flag-of-no-nation

Xiaojun first sees Mi Lan's photo through a military spyglass that he has removed from the wall of her apartment, a telescopic image that creates a compelling but elusive sense of intimacy with this phantasm [017]. The spyglass magically opens a world once barred to him: peering through it out the apartment window, to his mischievous delight he spies none other than Teacher Hu, flirting in the courtyard with another teacher, and relieving himself in an open-air privy. Then with the telescope to his eye, Xiaojun surveils Mi Lan's room like captured territory, spinning about in a circle so that the details of the room race past the eye, and for an instant a face spins past, a female face gazing back at him — visible only for two-thirds of a second, seventeen DVD frames, and heavily sequence-edited to prolong it to this length [018]. Startled, he breaks his spin, jerks his head up and away from the glass, and steps back in alarm. Caught in his trespass, surveilled in his surveillance, he looks about quickly to locate the figure looking at him, just as a clock chimes loudly to mark the critical moment and further unnerve him. But without the spyglass he cannot see her. Even as he stares ahead to where he guesses she

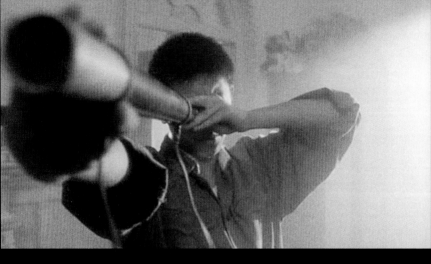

Photograph, seen through the looking glass

[019]

Bedstead, on close inspection

BODY VISIBLE

should be, he cannot see her there (not after forty-five more DVD frames, one and one-third seconds). Puzzled and more puzzled, he twice again takes up the spyglass to scan that area and there it is again (zipping by first in six DVD frames and then in seven, less than a quarter second each time).

Now, by its unvarying repetition, it appears this isn't a real flesh-and-blood girl but a fixed image of one, a compelling illusion. But each time after spying it, an unaided look at the wall where he thought the photo was tells him that now it isn't there (not after fifty more, then another thirty-seven DVD frames), just the illusion of an illusion. And after the third of these sightings is followed by the third failure to see, he rubs his eyes in disbelief at what is happening to him. The trickster is being tricked. Had he seen the girl's image on the wall or only in the spyglass? Finally he fixes the image in the glass and manages to track down the photograph only to trip at the last instant as he reaches out for it, for lack of range and broader perspective that this highly selective device impose. Is this device revealing a certain reality or is it deceiving him with its own seductive fiction; or is it bestowing an illusion of reality onto his own lies? Looking up from what turns out to be her bed (primal site of his ado-lescent fantasy — he has tripped over its threshold and over the threshold of romance), Xiaojun sees her smiling down upon him from the wall above, and at that moment a Western opera prelude begins to sound its lovely strains.[49] A piece of plain white gauze hangs over the girl's face, like a bridal veil, which he now raises in a state of anticipation. Then he backs away to enjoy her all the better from a distance, to caress her with his watchful eye peering through the spyglass.

A frame-by-frame examination reveals the reason he could not see the photograph with his naked eye: the photo really was not there. It is literally shown not to be there; there is only a wall, seen three times over to be blank [019], exactly where on a fourth and final viewing the photograph comes to "be." The magic lens not only reveals a visible spectacle; like Alice's looking glass, it makes the spectral visible. How, then, did the photograph come to "be there"? Was it ever really there, or is the audience's reading of the narra-tive being absorbed into a flawed and ill-fated authorial fantasy, a construct that will later unravel, deconstructed by an author who tells as the romance finally falls apart that:

44

My emotions changed my memories, which have in turn played with me and betrayed me. It got me all mixed up to the point where I can't distinguish between true and false. Now I suspect that the first time I met Mi Lan was fabricated. Actually, I never met her on the road.... I was never that familiar with Mi Lan. I never got familiar with Mi Lan. In fact, I never really knew her.... I started telling the story wishing to be sincere, yet my determined efforts have turned into lying. I can't give up at this point can I? No, no, and you wouldn't want me to, either.... So I'll continue our story, never mind whether it's the truth.[50]

Perhaps he has merely confused Mi Lan with another of his gang's girlfriends; maybe she really doesn't exist:

Heavens! Is Mi Lan the girl in the photograph? And whatever happened to Yu Beipei? Maybe she and Mi Lan were the same person? I don't dare think about it.

By the time of his telling it, Xiaojun is fully aware of the fragility of memory, truth, and history. "How hard it is to keep your promises!" he exclaims. "True honesty is impossible." He is fully in step with the modern psychologist's realization that memory is not a simple imprint-and-recall system but an ongoing work of construction and reconstruction[51] and that those who realize this best are those who are best able to exploit it for their own ends.[52] In real life, "truth" is hard or impossible to recover. In cinema, it can be recovered but only by violating the nature of the medium, turning the moving image into a series of still frames, reducing cinematography to photography.[53] Yet as we shall see, the makers of this film will do this for us themselves. In the meantime, the audience is swept along with the story, temporarily forgetting, as audiences do, that the story (true or false) is not really that of Ma Xiaojun (whether young and deceptive, as we see him on the screen; or older and forgetful as we hear him, the voiced-over narrator relating it all in the form of a flashback) but an author's tale told for an author's own adult purposes, using children and childhood for the occasion of faulty memory, emotional instability, and cultural confusion.[54]

If this memory has been manufactured, then we already have seen to what end and what it represents in the overlapping realms of romance, politics, and what Mao, as the most lavish of modern Chinese image-makers, called "revolutionary romanticism." Xiaojun falls in love not with Mi Lan but with the image itself, magnified and manipulated by wishful thinking and strange memory. It is also quite unstable. The second time Xiaojun returns secretly to her apartment, he prostrates himself before the icon, turns the bed into an altar of romance, and worships there a stray hair from her head that he finds. By that time, the romantic image is already linked to the political sphere and female linked to male by a pair of flags that newly appear there [020], held high by the picture frame as if by Mi Lan herself. One of these flags is the Chinese national flag, but the other belongs to no nation. It *could be* the flag of Czechoslovakia (fig. 13), but the positioning of its colors is wrong.[55] The image of Chinese and Czech flags flying side by side was actually printed on a Chinese postage stamp celebrating the tenth anniversary of the 1948 Communist "liberation" of Czechoslovakia (fig. 14). A similar juxtaposition occurs in a Chinese poster [of the previous year, with the Czech flag just below the Chinese flag amid a host of Communist country flags emblazoned on a flower pot sprouting bright red blossoms (fig. 15). But by "now" — the cinematic time of this event being located in the mid-1970s[56] — the relationship between China and the Soviet bloc was so antagonistic that nothing was left to celebrate and this flag could well have been misremembered.[57] Jiang Wen says that this constructed bit of misinformation was not quite so specific: "My art designer just put something together, arbitrarily."[58] These same two flags first appear in the immediately preceding scene, where Ma Xiaojun, Teacher Hu, and a group

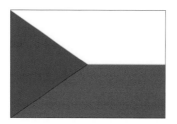

Figure 13 Czechoslovakian national flag.
Figure 14 Chinese postage stamp with flags of China and Czechoslovakia, 1958.
Figure 15 Unknown artist, "Long Live the United Socialist Nations," 1957. From "Propaganda posters," <debrisson .free.fr/maoism .html>.

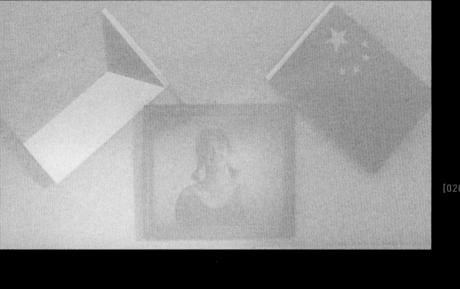

[020]

[021]

Diplomat of no nation

of Beijing children, well-scrubbed, rouge-cheeked, and purged momentarily of their hooliganism, wave garlands and paired Chinese and no-nation flags at a state-sponsored rally to welcome the entourage of black limousines of some visiting ambassador-of-no-nation; each car speeding by in a blur also sports these two flags, virtually impossible to see except frame by frame, at a moment when they have yet to acquire meaning [021]. Perhaps subsequent to this, Xiaojun himself has attached these flags to Mi Lan's photograph, at least in his mixed-up memory. Representing not a nation but a state of confusion, this constructed flag functions like calligrapher–book artist Xu Bing's *Book from the Sky*, with some 3,000 unreadable pseudocharacters designed to sow the seeds of cultural destabilization, each character of which the artist had to painstakingly make sure did not accidentally correspond to any of the 40,000 plus recorded Chinese characters, however obvious or obscure (fig. 16).[59]

Clearly, this cinematographic detail, set at a level beyond the capacity of any ordinary film audience to process, this minute demonstration of an absolute dedication to visual artistry and exactitude that seeks no applause, is intentionally inaccurate and designed to confirm Xiaojun's misremembrance of things. What, then is achieved by this carefully staged uncertainty? If the allegorical mode serves us well at this time, the fantasy relationship between Mi Lan and Ma Xiaojun parallels that of Mao and his idolaters, and is celebrated under a question mark about the reliability of "knowledge" that designates the uncertain and fragile relationship between the Party and the people.

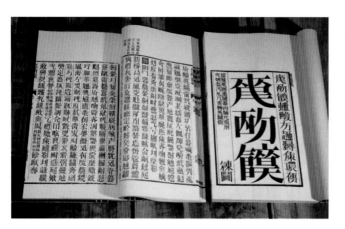

Figure 16 Xu Bing, *Book from the Sky*, exhibition installation, National Gallery, Beijing, February 1989. From Britta Erickson, *The Art of Xu Bing: Words Without Meaning, Meaning Without Words*, 34.

Naked hypocrisy

In addition to the apartments Xiaojun has invaded in secret, he joins a score of young friends on a more penetrating invasion that exposes the venality of the older generation. As the other children are being indoctrinated outdoors with a nighttime screening of *Red Detachment of Women* and *Lenin in 1918*,[60] Xiaojun and his companions sneak indoors to discover that the elder cadres there are watching quite a different film. This turns out to be an imported B-grade nudie with white women exposing white flesh [022]. As with so much of the film, the misbehavior might pass as light humor. What the moment reveals, however, is official hypocrisy. As the children are discovered in the cadres' midst, the film is stopped and the cadres' fun comes to an end. A senior official and his young, attractive female companion rise to explain that the cadres are merely criticizing the film's "extreme poison," lest the Chinese youth be led astray by it [023]. The children take this explanation in stride without a trace of doubt, which speaks to the gullibility of the times, the ready submission to the claims of those in authority. This is *not* a trivial event: here the narrative finger points to the source of its own deceptions — straight from Party sources comes the Original Lie. The cadres might as well have told the children, "This woman isn't naked."[61]

Romance takes flight, the romantic flyer becomes an animal

Infatuated with Mi Lan, Xiaojun imagines himself willing to die for her, is prepared to fly through the air trying, and deludes himself into thinking he has succeeded. Showing off for Mi Lan the first time he introduces her to his gang, Xiaojun scales a dangerously tall smokestack, many stories tall, only to fall down the middle of it [024]. As his friends watch in horror, he emerges from the bottom covered with soot, evidently saved from death by upward drafts within the funnel. Miraculously, then, he crawls out, proclaiming his heroism as one who has learned how to fly. His soot-blackened face, like Western-style blackface minstrelsy, a thin disguise, seems to reference the theater and especially the clowns (*chou*) of Chinese opera [025]. How appropriate that his nickname among friends, which they call out at this time, is "Monkey," the greatest of theatrical clowns and comic acrobats, magicians and tricksters. But behind the mask lies the same person, hiding the truth that there was

B-grade movie

[022]

[023]

Cadres

[024]

[025]

no magic in this event, no great or admirable achievement, just dumb luck that kept him alive despite his youthful foolishness. This is not the face of the magical Monkey after all, just the monkey-like face of mischief. Yet here, as in Corneille's *L'Illusion*, reality becomes confused with theatricality, exposing participants and observers alike to the subtleties of mass deception. Like Corneille, as Alcandre draws his deception to a close, Jiang Wen from this point on begins an unmasking process, gradually lifting the curtain, not on the stage but on the staging.

A wine bottle un-breaks, narration unwinds

The collapse and reconfiguration of Xiaojun's pretensions to narrative honesty comes in one of the most astonishing moments in modern Chinese cinema. At a joint birthday party for Xiaojun and Liu Yiku,[62] his fellow gang member and archrival for Mi Lan's affections, Xiaojun's adolescent jealousy boils over and gives way to a bodily assault [026]. He angrily smashes a wine bottle and attacks Liu Yiku with it, repeatedly stabbing him, over and over, twenty-five times in all, until the audience begins to realize something very peculiar is happening, that something has gone wrong not just with the event but with the narrative itself. The stabbing becomes mechanical, and Liu Yiku is not hurt. Then, as Liu himself visibly comes to realize this, he looks strangely at the hand that stabs and then scans the set, and as the background sounds become muted and finally silent, Liu turns briefly toward the camera as if to ask the director, "Okay, what really *is* happening here?" At this point, the film editor freezes the cinematic image [027] and Xiaojun in a narrative voice-over tells the audience:

> *Ha-ha!... Don't believe any of it. I never was this brave or heroic. I have kept swearing to tell the story truthfully, but no matter how strong my wish to tell the truth, all kinds of things have gotten in the way, and I sadly realize that I have no way to return to reality.*[63]

Casting doubt on whether he really knew Mi Lan at all, he begins to untell his story, and during his soliloquy the stabbing begins all over again, twenty-five more stabs, although this time — not obvious at first — the sequence takes place in reverse as the film is played backwards, unstab by unstab, time

[026]

[027]

"Ha-ha! I was never this brave."

reversing itself and the narrative unwinding until the wine begins to refill a reconstituted bottle.

If the audience is astonished at such an unlikely turn, it should realize by now that it has been taken in, not just by this singular scene but by *everything* that has come before. Henceforth, nothing is to be believed, no more than spilt wine can be put back into an un broken bottle. In his book *The Double-Screen: Medium and Representation in Chinese Painting*, Wu Hung discusses the semiotics of *trompe l'œil* paintings within paintings, of "layered surfaces and spaces," as the turning of simile into metaphor, illusion into illusion-ism, voyeurism into fetishism. Through this "perfect illusionism," this "magic" (*huan*), "the artist is able to deceive not only the viewer's eye but his mind.... The viewer is able to take what is painted as real."[64] Of course, one could argue to the contrary, that what this illusion*ism* reveals to the viewer, as it does to Wu Hung, is the illusion*istic* nature of art, the magician's tricks, a self-reflexive artistry. This is exactly what happens at this moment in *Heat of the Sun*, when the medium of cinematography turns into photography, motion (*kinema*) is stopped, and change is turned into mere repetition. Suddenly, the frame reap-pears, the magic of the magic lantern is revealed, the trajectory of the narra-tive is brought to a standstill, and the film is no longer told-fiction but a truth-ful discourse on telling. As in *L'Illusion Comique*, the audience is liable to be even more stunned by the revelation of deception than it was by deception itself. With the subtle use of repeated film frames in the earlier schoolroom setting, we were tricked and so who even noticed? Here we are untricked, to much greater effect.

Significantly, the reconstitution of the wine bottle is not entirely complete, the story is not fully retracted, when the film sequence freezes again and the narrator tells us that he is not yet done with his tale, and we would not want him to be either. Even if he is not to be believed, there is still more to be said: he has yet to make his main point (and, indeed, he will not make it until after the viewer thinks the film is over, with nothing left but film credits and an unex-pected bit of black-and-white footage seen as a cinematic coda). And there is more, still, for memory to erase.

The hero castrated, the heroine raped — almost

Xiaojun's failure to rise to the level of heroic battle except in his fertile imagination is followed by two scenes that further emasculate him and spell his romantic doom. In the first, riding his bicycle at night through a driving rain [028], as he approaches Mi Lan's home he plunges into a construction hole and is injured in his most sensitive part. The psychological overtones of this erotic plunge are enormous, and he imagines (for the audience to see) in great, romantic detail Mi Lan coming to his rescue with loving arms, but by now he is well aware of his own delusions and the chaos of his own memories. "Is it possible," he asks himself, "that what happened that night wasn't real? But the part where I was injured still hurts!" As if to assure himself that his memory is more than half true and that his masculinity is intact, Xiaojun makes one last attempt to bodily claim Mi Lan for himself, to keep the heroic dream alive, bicycling off the next day to Mi Lan's apartment , where he proceeds to rape her [029]. Or at least he attempts to do so, for her superior will and his own bodily injury (real or imagined) now stand in the way. This is the bed that once served as altar for his devotion to the red-swimsuit photograph, but the photo is no longer there and the event is now driven not by desire but disgust and self-loathing. In terms of theatrical genealogy, this vengeful scene extends into a new, Chinese generation of artistic expression that blue-blooded lineage of destructive intent born with Shylock's signature line, "Hates any man the thing he would not kill?," which Oscar Wilde (theatricalizing his own erotic downfall) inverted in his "Ballad of Reading Gaol":

> Yet each man kills the thing he loves,
> By each let this be heard,
> Some do it with a bitter look,
> Some with a flattering word.
> The coward does it with a kiss,
> The brave man with a sword![65]

Wilde's version casts more light on Ma Xiaojun's limitations than on his potency: Xiaojun does it only with a forcible kiss, for he has no sword and only an injured part — he is all bravado and no bravery. Mi Lan is spared but she

[028]

[029]

is left naked, exposed to the camera and the audience — breasts, nipples and all, a rare and risky venture for a mainland Chinese film.[66]

The longing for affectionate intimacy can now only be approximated through intimate violence. Imagining that she once desired him but now has betrayed him instead, Xiaojun reduces Mi Lan to an object of shame and disgust, the final rupture of his constructed myth in that awful, overheated summer. But Mi Lan proves the stronger and survives Xiaojun's clumsy efforts to overthrow her, just as the Communist Party survived the youth upheaval of 1989, which similarly started with the genuine desire for the body politic but ended in a violent failure to penetrate the inner sanctum of the state. Ma Xiaojun's failure shames him even more than it does her.

Betrayed by the collective body, the hero crucified

As the summer of his passion lengthens and then wanes, Xiaojun has lost Mi Lan's affections — if he ever had them. Defeated and deflated, Xiaojun returns to the scene before the crime, to the swimming pool, where he makes his failure and his incompetence public for all to see. Once before, at the height of his passion for Mi Lan, he dove down a chimney shaft and miraculously survived; now, he is tempted to match the superb diving skills of his rival, to replicate his own earlier flight, this time from the (very) high board of a swimming pool. But his slow and awkward ascent to the heights demonstrates what he already knows by now, that it cannot be done. No miracle occurs to resurrect his hopes. The result is an ungainly, unmanly, and disastrously embarrassing failure. With this, all of his romantic pretensions collapse. Defeated, he swims to the edge of the pool, to the outstretched hands of his companions all lined up, carefully posed, ready to help him from the water [030] [031]. Only, as he comes within reach they shove him under with their feet, time and again, a humiliation set to the broken-hearted pulsation of Mascagni's "Intermezzo Sinfonico" from his opera *Cavalliera Rusticana* (*Rustic Chivalry*), whose tale parallels Xiaojun's disillusionment, betrayal, and crushed romance.[67] The collective body, the community as he once knew it, now threatens to destroy him. In the end, he is left floating on the water in a crucified pose [032]. As the finale to a teenage romance, it is suitably overdramatized. As a metaphor, an embodiment of the people's betrayal by the Party and of China's loss of faith

[030]

[031]

Hands

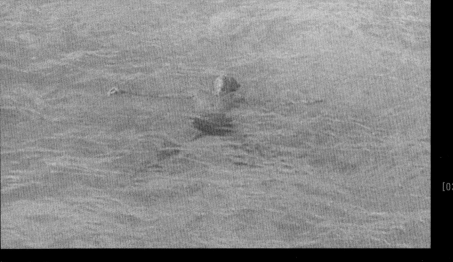

[032]

"Crucified"

in her glorious Revolution — in her young, red Party, in herself — Xiaojun's tale of self-deception finally unravels, and a deeply moving tragedy is arrived at, step-by-step, as a descent from initial hope, adolescent naiveté, and comedic impulse into emotional dusk and narrative darkness. But a crucifixion, more than a mere martyrdom, is a prelude of something yet to come, a glorious, mysterious resurrection, an utter transfiguration.

The present disfigured by its own idiocy

There is but one scene left in the film, an epilogue executed to the accompaniment of overlaid film credits and set in present-day Beijing. Xiaojun is grown up, and the young actor Xia Yu is replaced by none other than the film's director, Jiang Wen himself. The scene, transformed, was described by the adult Ma Xiaojun-as-narrator at the outset of the film: "Beijing has changed so fast. In twenty years, it's become a modern city. Almost nothing is the way I remembered it." Radical change, undoubtedly, has contributed to the instability of narrative memory. But as we shall see, it is the nature of *this* change, more than the unstable nature of memory *per se*, that Jiang Wen's film is interested in. Ironically, unlike so many films in which the past is coded by presentation in black-and-white that becomes color saturated as it rolls into the present (Hou Hsiao-hsien's *Good Men, Good Women*, for example[68]), here the falsified past — the era of false hope — is shown in color and the present is desaturated into shades of black and white. It is as if the past, however badly misconstrued, is gauged to have had greater vitality than the present, which in grim contrast can only be seen as a satirical comment on what this self-delusion has wrought. Comedy returns, as it did in Corneille's *L'Illusion Comique*, in the form of black humor disguising tragedy. Xiaojun, once disgraced and with illusions now discarded, is now shown cruising Beijing with his old buddies in a white stretch limousine, driving (significantly) past Tiananmen and drinking hard liquor as they noisily poke their heads through the open sunroof of their car [033]. As bad now as they were in their youth, what do they suddenly see from those bygone days? The neighborhood idiot known to them as Gulunmu ("Old Hunk-of-Wood") [034] from the piece of wood, now, as long ago shoved between his legs like an elevated penis, with which he stumbles along the street, unaffected by self-consciousness or sense of shame.

Traditionally in China, abnormal children were a source of embarrassment to the family, who kept them hidden from public view.[69] Beijing differs a bit in this, and Ma Xiaojun and friends actually went out of their way to defend Gulunmu from predators. But whereas in his youth, the only words spoken by the imbecile were his name mispronounced as "Ooloomoo" or "Ooba" [035], now as they shout at him in recognition and derision he shouts back a new word at them, given in English subtitles as "Sha B. — Cretin!" Perhaps being something of a cretin himself, he recognizes them for what they are, with an amazing, single phrase by which he defines, or defiles, the entire story in shades of vulgarity and decadence.

But exactly what does this redirecting of labels indicate? Who and what does this carload of wealthy men embody, in their dapper business suits, behaving as foolish little boys? Nothing other, I would suggest, than what we see: the sons of the revolutionary Communism's elite cadres, favored by inheritance, now grown up, rich, and powerful — once the target of Tiananmen's student demonstrations, now constituting today's economic ruling elite. Devoid of a sincere Communist faith, which they lost in those days of summer youth, they now rule without it. Like Gulunmu, they embody an embarrassing cultural disfigurement, a loss of intelligent meaning, a confusion between the private and public realms. Like him they share a half-witted understanding of social morality, and with Gulunmu they share an embarrassing readiness to masturbate self-indulgently in public.[70] Literally, *sha bi* translates as "stupid cunt," casting Xiaojun and his companions — today's ruling elite — in thoroughly sexualized terms, not only charged with idiocy but their masculinity attacked, stripped of the ideological aura that surrounded and held their forebears aloft in an earlier generation and reduced now to the grossest physicality, a bodily part suggesting here the pursuit of self-satisfaction and self-replication.[71] On this closing scene, the symbolic stage curtain descends.

Just how this transformation from past to present, from a generation of ardent Maoists to one of self-serving capitalist roaders, took place without a change in the composition of the ruling elite, is not explored or explained, except by a conspicuous avoidance. This, after all, is the greatest of China's modern mysteries, genuine stage magic. On another level, however, it is no mystery at all: those spoiled children, in their parents' large, well-furnished

[033]

[034]

Limousine and Gulunmu

Young Gulunmu

[035]

[036]

Adult Liu Yiku

apartments and swimming pools, in their summer of fun when the rest of the nation was embroiled in the hard work of "making revolution," those sons and daughters of a favored few make it all too clear that there was no social equality in the first place.

Epilogue: the past disembodied, nostalgia embodied

From a certain perspective, this last scene of the film embodies the devastating logic of the whole, a portrait of a society without direction, cruising about in style on a chill winter's day, comfortably but mindlessly, and without purpose. But upon reflection, equally conspicuous here is something portrayed in terms of bodily absence. Color is absent here, as is the warmth of the summer sun, and so is the girl-in-red, the colorful Mi Lan. In his final voiced-over narrative, Xiaojun accounts for the fate of his fellow gang members of that summer. Liu Yiku, his handsome rival, will go mad during the China's embarrassing 1979 border war with Vietnam (the mere mention of which, with special reference to Chinese casualties, might not have escaped the censors' oversight); yet he appears in the final scene [036] as the most mindless one of those riding around in the white limousine, and as the clearest link to the idiot Gulunmu.[72] As for Mi Lan, Xiaojun tells us, "two months later [she] stopped hanging out with us." She does not appear again, and her absence at the end is a resonant reminder of what was but is no more, just like Mao himself. As such, *In the Heat of the Sun* joins other Chinese-language films like *Suzhou River* and *Good Men, Good Women* in which disembodiment is used to mark the collapse of a unifying ideological purpose and the disappearance of elevating patriotism from the lives of a younger generation.[73] The males in the limousine are notably deprived of a female to long for, idealize, and idolize, and they are left with only an idiot to leer at.

In the Heat of the Sun was made during the height of the so-called Mao Craze or Mao Fever when, in the aftermath of the Tiananmen "incident," the harsh realities of the Cultural Revolution were forgiven in behalf of a longing for strong leadership and a unifying national direction. This later, foolish period—not just the former, crazy one—may be the primary target of the film's criticism, of its critique by indirection: by disembodiment, one might say. Nostalgia, of course, is a weaker phenomenon than ideological fervor, and by the end of the film, Maoism — like Mi Lan, like the youth of Xiaojun's generation — was long beyond real recovery. By the early 1990s, Mao's "presence" was but a distorted memory, nostalgically embodied in the trivialized format of wrist watches, cigarette lighters that played the revolutionary tune of "The East is Red," and automotive safety medallions like the one hung conspicuously on the windshield of Xiaojun's 1994-model white Lincoln limousine [038].[74] It was an era when China had more than just begun to lose its Chineseness but wouldn't let go of it and could only hold onto it by the most curious, often banal means, like the trendy restaurant near the Beijing airport that features a donkey circling a grain mill that grinds no grain but "creates a bucolic atmosphere to attract customers" (fig. 17). What we have, then, in this film is not some nostalgic eroticization of politics but rather the politicization of erotica: in other words, anti-nostalgia.

The particulars of *In the Heat of the Sun* distinguish it in many regards from most Chinese-language films, but in a broader sense the "language" itself is not unique. It shares a subtlety of reference, a readiness of allegorical convertability, and a comfortable familiarity with analogical rhetoric that help define the traditional language, both visual and verbal, of premodern Chinese art and literature. It is a language in which a horse is not just a horse, a tree can be more a person than a tree, a mountain can represent a historical morality play, where a lovely plant can be a palace lady and a lonely palace

Figure 17 Yang Shen, *Creating a Bucolic Atmosphere to Attract Customers*, black-and-white photograph, 2002. From Wang Huangsheng and Hu Wugong, eds., *Zhongguo renben, jishi zai dangdai: Humanism in China, A Contemporary Record of Photography*, 323.

馬小軍　　夏　　雨
（童年）
（成年）　韓　　冬
　　　　　姜　　文

lady can be a dejected politician — a carefully formulated and distinctively Chinese language developed down through the centuries to maintain a high level of dialogue among an educated, politically privileged elite while avoiding political culpability in a highly censorial society and, accordingly, through increasing refinements of expression to define and intellectually cultivate that minority while excluding a far larger majority from comprehension and thus participation in this dialogue.[75] This use and even an awareness of this exclusionary language persists only barely in our own time, and only among a remnant or as a vestige of that ancient intellectual cadre that once ruled China as the scholar-elite, overthrown in modern times by the downfall of dynastic rule and the rise of mass culture. Jiang Wen's use of this esoteric language in the cinematic narratives of *Heat of the Sun* and *Devils on the Doorstep*, and the intensity of his reliance on it in details scarcely noticeable by an ordinary film-going audience, suggest the address of his films to an audience other than the ordinary one that might well be satisfied by viewing *In the Heat of the Sun* as a coming-of-age romance-disappointment, an audience that might represent an imagined communion of the filmmakers with the lofty artistic traditions of China's past, or perhaps an audience of one, Jiang Wen himself.

In the Heat of the Sun begins, in color, with a solid, colossal, sunlit sculpture of the Chairman [037], looked up to from below and set to the strains of revolutionary music:

In the raging storm of revolution
The soldier's hearts turn toward the sun.
Oh Chairman Mao, Chairman Mao,
We want to express our ardour to you....
Your brilliant thoughts are like dew and sunlight.

It ends colorlessly, drained of youthful hope and passion, with the Chairman reduced to a small flat photograph [038], enframed as the God of Traffic Safety, dangling helplessly from a rear-viewing mirror. ∎

BODY AND THE BEAST
Devils on the Doorstep

Devils on the Doorstep (*Guizi laile*) DIRECTOR: Jiang Wen SCREENPLAY: Jiang Wen, Shu Ping,
Liu Xing, Shi Jianquan, Li Haiying ORIGINAL TEXT: You Fengwei, novella *Shengcun* (*Survival*)
CINEMATOGRAPHY: Gu Changwei FILM EDITING: Folmer Wiesinger, Zhang Yifan ORIGINAL MUSIC:
Cui Jian, Li Haiying, Liu Xing ART DIRECTION: Cai Weidong PRODUCERS: Dong Ping, Jiang Wen,
Zheng Quangang STUDIOS: Asia Union Film and Entertainment, China Film Coproduction
Corporation CAST: Jiang Wen (Ma Dasan), Jiang Hongbo (Yu'er), Kagawa Teruyuki (Hanaya
Kosaburo), Yuan Ding (Dong Hanchen), Sawada Kenya (Captain Sakatsuka Inokichi), Xi Zi (Liu
Wang, village elder), Cong Zhijun (Grandfather, Yu'er's late husband's father), Chen Lianmei
(Aunt), Chen Qiang ("One-Stroke" Liu), David Wu (Major Gao), Cai Weidong (Er Bozi), Zhou
Haizhao (Little Thresher), Miyaji Yoshitomo (Koji Nonomura), James Mayfield (US marine),
Abram Sauer (US Marine), Li Haibin ("Me") **Black-and-white and color 139 minutes 2000**

[039]

You really become that person once you put on the khaki uniform, you put on the glasses, you take the nightstick, and you act the part.
Guard Hellman, in the 1971 Stanford Prison Experiment[77]

The creatures outside looked from pig to man, and from man to pig, and from pig to man again; but already it was impossible to say which was which.
George Orwell, *Animal Farm*[78]

In their first film together, *In the Heat of the Sun*, director Jiang Wen and cinematographer Gu Changwei staked out a particular place on the contemporary stage alongside a host of fellow Chinese artists. Painters, photographers, and cinematographers, theirs are carefully rehearsed scenes, planned and posed, of slightly dark, tongue-in-cheek humor that satirizes the newest incarnation of the "New China" in the throes of its adolescent coming-of-age. In *Heat of the Sun*, like some fair-skinned smiling child morphing into a pimply and somewhat pretentious youth, wisening up but not yet quite wise (more like a wise-guy, a *pizi*), irony and satire rise to undermine the old standards — the typical, the canonical (*dianxing*), the ideological; the self-certain if naive scientific materialism of Marx, Mao, and their heroic vanguard gives way to the marketplace materialism of Deng Xiaoping, his successors, and his cheeky detractors.

Like Gu Changwei's cinematography for *Heat of the Sun*, the photography of Hong Hao exemplifies this mode (fig. 18).[79] Like Ma Xiaojun parading about in his father's uniforms, Hong Hao appears in most of his "own" photographs as a poseur, not a militant Maoist but a consummate consumer. As elegantly mannered as a fine Bronzino portrait but modeled more contemporaneously

Figure 18 Hong Hao, *Mr. Hong, Please Come In*, color photograph, 1998. From Petr Nedoma and Chang Tsong-zung, *A Strange Heaven: Contemporary Chinese Photography*, 61.

on trendy advertising that targets the connoisseur of deluxe products, in *Mr. Hong, Please Come In* Hong Hao advertises the good life with a gathering of exotic goods that speak to the inculcation of global desires: Ionic and Corinthian columns; Gothic, South Asian, and eighteenth-century pseudo-Egyptian temple models; American cigar-store Indians and African sculptures; tribal pole-masks that frame Hong Hao like a chieftain — nothing left out and everything an imitation of the real thing, like the calla lilies (reaching up to a pair of carved angels) that seem to mock the sacred Christian lily — not to mention, as part of this well-organized culture-clutter, a canine status symbol whose posture carefully complements his master's own; a mirror that emphasizes specularity, artificiality (there are no reflections of the flowers or tribal arrows), and the multiplication of things; and above all else, the cross-cultural collection of stylized graphic fonts and scripts spread over the surface (referencing, perhaps, not only advertising copy but also the inscribed Chinese painting). In a pose that is studiously off-center but exquisitely self-conscious and supercilious, looking up from the would-be absorption in his reading and his culture of collecting, with a diffident, gently turned hand to cheek, Hong Hao primarily advertises himself — self-centeredness itself. Along the upper border, small characters tell us that "A gentle tone readily allows Mr. Hong to enter a peaceful reverie." The exaggerated "PLEASE" in "Come in Mr. Hong," "*Qing jinru*," drips with an affectation that parodies the entire thing in the leading languages of two hemispheres. Such is the critique, the mockery of an age, that turns the photograph's shallowness into critical depth, as with *Heat of the Sun's* coming-of-age romance, while threatening through its own studied cleverness to draw the depth back into its own shallowness. Setting his sights on mass culture and mass media, as it turns out, what has been appropriated here are not just gathered items but the entire photograph, taken intact from a commercial photograph (fig. 19), into which Hong Hao has digitally inserted himself: a critique on ownership and one-upsmanship.

Figure 19
Christopher Irion, untitled color photograph, ca. 1992.

Figure 20 Hei Ming, *Workers' Dining Hall in Zichang, Shanxi*, black-and-white photograph, 1985. Guangdong Museum of Art. From Wang Huangsheng and Hu Wugong, eds., *Zhongguo renben, jishi zai dangdai: Humanism in China, A Contemporary Record of Photography*, 566.

This genre of photography, a first cousin of cinematography, has gained the status of "hip" and succeeded in advertising its way into international acclaim.[80] Far less successful in China has been that genre which dominated Western photography throughout much of the twentieth century, the artistically inspired documentary photo that gives the appearance at least of being unstaged, of capturing through patience, through having the knack and the technical know-how, the fleeting and unrepeatable moment or display of personal character, and which in contrast to painting and composed or composite photography that, in Edward Weston's words, has "tried to improve nature by imposition," instead "prove[s] that nature offers an endless number of perfect 'compositions,' — order everywhere."[81] Such a work is photojournalist Hei Ming's 1985 image of a crude workers' dining hall in rural north China (fig. 20) where, after everyone else has eaten, the bowls have all been washed and hung up to dry, and the cook himself finally takes his turn.[82] (Perhaps: the single frame does not provide its own narration.) The endlessly varied disposition of crockery, like the composition of repeated fruits in Muqi's famous *Six Persimmons* painting, only multiplied, is matched by the singular angle of the diner's own bowl and the bowl-like Muslim skullcap on his head (which, beyond the visual, conveys further suggestions about food and its preparation). The numerous circles and ovals are paired with the rectangles of the doors, framed window, and dried bricks. The complete ensemble may well have been something that the photographer waited long for, perhaps even urged on, lit in his own way and cropped. Just how the bowls are hung is mystifying, and the photograph is better for not revealing the mechanism. But the subject matter remains essentially "found" and deserves, as such, to be found critically as a work of "fine art."

The presence of a camera, everywhere, has its own effect. But in China, now far more than in the West, cultivated by centuries of formal portraiture, the stronger tendency is toward the artificial, toward posing in ways that deny photographers the opportunity for a candid capture (fig. 21). The urge to "find" could lead Edward Weston, famously, to photograph a porcelain latrine (his 1925 *Excusado*) (fig. 22), then exalt its sinuous grace — "every sensuous curve of the 'human figure divine' but minus imperfections" — and liken its "swelling, sweeping forward movement of finely progressing contours" to the Nike of Samothrace.[83] In contrast to this, Susan Sontag has argued that

> In China taking pictures is always a ritual; it always involves posing and, necessarily, consent. Someone who "deliberately stalked people who were unaware of his intention to film them" was depriving people and things of their right to pose, in order to look their best.... Generally, what people do with the camera is assemble for it, then line up in a row or two.... Sports photographs show the team as a group, or only the most stylized balletic movements of play.... The Chinese resist the photographic dismemberment of reality. Close-ups are not used...the object is always photographed straight on, centered, evenly lit, and in its entirety.[84]

Figure 21 Li Dan, *Taking a Souvenir Photograph of Travelers in the Wenshu Courtyard, Chengdu*, black-and-white photograph, 1983. Guangdong Museum of Art. From Wang Huangsheng and Hu Wugong, eds., *Zhongguo renben, jishi zai dangdai: Humanism in China, A Contemporary Record of Photography*, 393.

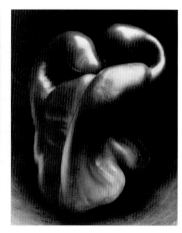

Figure 22 Left: Edward Weston, *Excusado*, black-and-white photograph, 1925. Center: Edward Weston, *Nude*, 1936. Right: Edward Weston, *Pepper*, 1930. From Gilles Mora, ed., *Edward Weston: Forms of Passion*, 109, 223, 171, respectively.

Sontag, in 1973, remained unaware of Chinese experimental photography of the Republican period, an artistic movement cut short by war and revolution[85] and had little inkling of the cultural changes that lay just around the corner. The Chinese aesthetic, she concluded, "is the characteristic visual taste of those at the first stage of camera culture, when the image is defined as something that can be stolen from its owner" and derives from a "moral order of space that preclude[s] the photographic way of seeing."[86]

Sontag also wrote that "the history of photography could be recapitulated as the struggle between two different imperatives: beautification, which comes from the fine arts, and truth telling," which she describes as derived from the sciences, from nineteenth-century literary models, and finally from independent journalism.[87] Hei Ming's work doesn't struggle but fulfills both imperatives. If Chinese photography was ever "behind" in this genre, it has certainly begun to "catch up," or at least the cultural divide has now largely been spanned; and already, the more alert contemporary Chinese critics have spoken to the cultural subjectivity and historical fluidity of self-presentation, as both documented by and affected by visual technology.[88]

Less "artistic," perhaps, as a formal composition, but no less telling in content is Wang Fuchun's candid photograph (fig. 23) of a grandmother and grandson in a traveling compartment on a train, in 1993, both of them markedly aware of the camera but unstaged in their action and their reaction to a child-hood erection, which the arched-back boy appears almost to pander to the photographer. The older woman responds with a facial display that demands interpretation: is she surprised (at her discovery of this biological phenomenon), embarrassed (if not by the child, then by the presence of the photographer recording her own response), delighted (at the prospect of future progeny that the child's gesture portends)? These alternatives are not simply hers alone but are bound up with acculturated norms, such that a Western audience, despite its daily exposure to sexualized imagery through a variety of entertainment and advertising media, might find the exhibition of such a photograph to be not merely a vulgar display but a moral and perhaps legal violation of the privacy rights of all children, whereas a Chinese audience, used to the daily parading about of bare-bottomed little boys and girls and doubly delighted by the birth and raising of boys, might be less troubled by the event itself than by its recording and public display. While the event may not shock, the photograph may. On deeper consideration, such an image may be more troubling than it is shocking. It dissipates the illusion of childhood innocence — and obstructs any viewing adult's pretense to the same. Conversely, it suggests that adults are but children. While it records nothing more than a simple physiological response (not yet sexual, hormonally driven; a full bladder will do it), it is a reminder that we are animals, bodily creatures, inescapably complex and often not in control of the mechanisms and drives that physically and psychologically

Figure 23 Wang Fuchun, *Amused Grandmother and her Grandson in a Sleeper Car of the Train from Lanzhou to Urumqi*, black-and-white photograph, 1993. Guangdong Museum of Art. From Wang Huangsheng and Hu Wugong, eds., *Zhongguo renben, jishi zai dangdai: Humanism in China, A Contemporary Record of Photography*, 244.

regulate our behavior. And it reminds us of the power of images, telling us that we may react most strongly, least rationally, to what we don't expect or understand, to what we don't want to see or don't want others to see. (The art historian can scarcely avoid thinking of related issues raised by Leo Steinberg's controversial but eminently humane classic *The Sexuality of Christ in Renaissance Art and Modern Oblivion*.[89])

It is *this* photographic genre — not of Hong Hao but of Hei Ming and Wang Fuchun — whose appearance Jiang Wen and Gu Changwei adapted for their next cinematic work, *Devils on the Doorstep*, a film that delights and offends equally, that mixes humor and horror with astonishing intensity, that presents humanity in all its complexity and saves the worst for the last [040]. So different visually from *Heat of the Sun* and its correlate in Hong Hao's *Please Come In*, which *look* contrived because they are all about contrivance, *Devils on the Doorstep* must work even harder to *not* look contrived, making every effort to not look like a studio film. It responds to a darker urge, attempting to appear as if cinematographer Gu Changwei, like Wang Fuchun on the train, was "just there," recording history as it happened in order for history itself, rather than the artists, to seem responsible for taking the audience farther into the darkness than most viewers care to go. Set in the rural north of China during the last months of Japan's brutal occupation, the film's imagery draws much of its visual character from actual photographic documentation now lodged in historical memory, from newsreels and simulacra of those events like the world-famous photo of a baby (fig. 24), bloodied and alone after

Figure 24 H.S. Wong, *Shanghai, South Station*, film frame, August 28, 1937. From John Faber, *Great News Photos and the Stories behind Them*, 74.

Little Thresher

the intense aerial bombardment of Shanghai's crowded South Station on August 28, 1937.[90]

Of course, even documentary photography may be subject to manipulation and doubt, including H.S. Wong's own work at the Shanghai railway station that day (figs. 24, 25).[91] And certainly *Devils'* historical mimesis is not for real, but it is carefully made to look like the spontaneous seizing of a fleeting reality.[92] Henri Cartier-Bresson, among the first to raise photojournalism to an artistic level, wrote in 1933,

> "Manufactured" or staged photography does not concern me. There are those who take photographs arranged beforehand and those who go out to discover the image and seize it. For me, the camera is a sketch book, an instrument of intuition and spontaneity, the master of the instant which — in visual terms — questions and decides simultaneously.... To take photographs is to hold one's breath when all faculties converge in the face of fleeting reality.[93]

This describes well the breathless aesthetic of Jiang Wen's and Gu Changwei's film. While *Devils on the Doorstep* is entirely manufactured, it contrives to seem otherwise. The trick of its carefully arranged pseudodocumentation is to stop reality in its flight, to stage the instant, to hide all traces of its manufacture.[94] In some ways it is as deceptive as *Heat of the Sun*, appearing to be the cinematic relative of Hei Ming and Wang Fuchun when in manufacture it is no less closely related to Hong Hao.[95]

Taiwanese film director Yang Dechang (Edward Yang) once described filmmakers as limited by public reception to either intense visuality or intense dialogue — a principle he intentionally violated in his films *A Confucian Confusion* (*Duli shidai*, 1994) and *Mahjong* (1996) in order to capture the effects of social and moral chaos brought about by Taiwan's "economic miracle."[96] In a manner distinctively reminiscent of films like Kurosawa's *Rashomon* (cinematographer Miyagawa Kazuo, 1950), Gu Changwei shot in black-and-white with high-contrast lighting, much of it extremely close-up and tightly framed in a way that reflects the forced intimacy of village life and the inability of helpless villagers to escape intruders from the outside and the situation imposed on them. In contrast to his early work in films like *King of the Children*, where

Figure 25 Unknown
photographer,
H.S. Wong and baby
at South Station,
Shanghai, August 28,
1937.

the scarcely moving camerawork had an incapacitating effect on characters
facing a seemingly unchangeable China, the camerawork in *Devils* moves at
a frenetic pace, if only to achieve the same ultimate effect, of showing people
getting nowhere despite their desperate efforts to move out of harm's way.
Devils is the visualization of an intense dialogue which, like a complex novel,
needs to be pondered slowly while it is read. Each of the characters plays a
culturally assigned role in the film's many-sided consideration of the coloniz-
ing process, obliged to question openly the reality and the unreality of the various possible trajectories, outcomes, or escapes that might result from their
collaboration or resistance. And yet, as in Yang Dechang's films, the forced
pace of *Devils on the Doorstep* prevents the film's characters from much of the
needed pondering, never allowing them enough time to think through their
predicament before being obliged to act and face the consequences, and it
sets the audience in the same quandary. As characters think aloud, argue
and interrupt one another — an enormous challenge for film editors Folmer
Wiesinger and Zhang Yifan — the camera shifts jarringly back and forth from
one anxious, uncertain face to another (see frames 050, 051). Faces and dialogue alike are set in the vernacular, hard-bitten, so unlike those in either
Chinese state propaganda or approved "entertainment" films and so inher-
ently dissident. The following examples illustrate the film's cinematic style,
its use of body in an acculturated context, and the ways in which these nego-
tiate between image and meaning.

How to execute an execution

Late in the film, one of the film's "middle characters" — a Chinese translator whom the film's main character has struggled to protect from one dire fate after another — is sentenced to be executed for collaboration with the enemy. And so the translator, Dong Hanchen, is summarily done away with by a bullet to the back of the head. Unlike state propaganda films in China, where government-engendered violence is kept discreetly off-screen,[97] nor accompanied by the splattering-of-blood and smoking-wounds aesthetic of violence-for-the-fun-of-it films from Hong Kong and the West, the event is carried out with a sudden forward acceleration that hurls the victim face down into the dust, in a mechanical dying that is over almost before it begins. Void of drama or any feeling at all, it is all the more brutal for the lack of it. Only, one striking detail lingers in the mind's eye: in front of the victim, as he flies forward, the bullet that passes through his skull kicks up the dust before him, sooner than he can land there [041] [042] [043] [044]. It is a shocking piece of cinematic "realism,"[98] one that seems to dispense with aesthetics in favor of "the thing itself," as if a return to that once-new industrial-age realism proclaimed long ago by Walt Whitman, whose "greatest poet" (as he wrote of himself)

> swears to his art, I will not be meddlesome, I will not have in my writing any elegance or effect.... I will have nothing hang in the way.... What I tell, I tell for precisely what it is.... What I experience or portray shall go from my composition without a shred of my composition.[99]

Of course, this execution is neither real documentation except in style and anything but artless, and like Whitman's self-awareness that hung like a curtain in the way of everything else, what the detail really documents is the film's thorough awareness of its own deepest intentions. Such fine detail does not happen casually — no bullet really passes through the victim's head — but like the scarcely noticed "Czech" flag in *Heat of the Sun*, it is carefully contrived. Jiang Wen provides some of the details:

> First, we constructed a metal head-gear with hair on top. Then, where the actor was going to fall, we dug up a hole and filled it with soft earth so when he fell forward he could do so safely and comfortably. Next, we carefully

82

calibrated how far in front of him to place the charge to get the effect of its shooting into the ground. Finally, we shot this sequence at only twenty or twenty-one frames per second [to be projected at the usual twenty-four frames per second, creating the time-lapse effect of the actor being hurled forward more rapidly]."[100]

The effect of this, both artificial and artful, is directed toward the emotions: ironically, to deprive this execution of its anticipated level of emotional reality — the horror of it — in order to achieve yet another level to which the entire film is dedicated — the horror of its having no horror! For the film audience, the instrumentation of death suddenly becomes more real than the emotional life of the victim. Those who have never observed a real shooting before may ponder, so *that* is how it happens, their attention drawn away from the one it has happened to. The victim, with whom the audience has already become familiar and not a little sympathetic, is suddenly a nobody, an incident, dispatched and forgotten. Like the gathered audience depicted within the scene, the film audience partakes in death as public spectacle, experiencing death as commonplace, lacking the mechanical agency by which to change the outcome of film or the moral agency by which to change their world. Thus, by a detail — and by many such gathered details — the film audience is brought to close ranks with a society desensitized to institutional brutality, deprived by years and centuries of oppression from without and within of the moral bearing or emotional impetus by which to right itself.

Film critic Xiao Peng describes the ends to which Jiang Wen went to perfect the artistic effect of realism even when not visible to the audience, exemplified by Jiang's uncompromising study of Japanese military uniforms for use in the film, done partly in Japan (at Tokyo's Yasukuni shrine) while casting, partly with the consultation of People's Liberation Army outfitters, and partly through documentary film. Xiao Peng concludes that "Jiang Wen sought not to be off by the slightest bit, so for example, when the military uniforms originally had four stitches per centimeter and the manufactured ones differed by one, then the whole thing was rejected." He quotes Jiang's associate director Zhao Yijun as saying that "Jiang Wen left on him the deeply carved impression, first of thoroughness, second of thoroughness, and third of thoroughness.

[041]

[042]

Hanchen executed

Because Jiang Wen's production put this thoroughness first, his results were first rate."[101] Peter Hessler adds, based on an interview with Jiang Wen:

> During the filming of *Devils on the Doorstep*, Jiang Wen refused to shoot out-takes. If a small part of a scene was unacceptable, he insisted on reshooting the entire thing from the beginning. In the film industry, this practice is unheard of, and Jiang Wen reportedly used every roll of Kodak black-and-white movie film that was available in China — five hundred thousand feet, or roughly five times the amount required for the average feature film.... The movie cost an estimated five million dollars, twice the original budget.[102]

Two lovers, naked, and a hidden warrior

Like *Heat of the Sun*, *Devils on the Doorstep* is vitally concerned with historical myth and falsification,[103] using cinematic techniques of unmasking and exposure. *Devils*, in particular, is concerned with labels and stereotypes: national, racial, and ethnic. Ma Xiaojun in *Heat of the Sun* is a dissimulator who despite his repeated confessions to that charge dwells in a world of illusions; *Devils'* Ma Dasan, played by director Jiang Wen himself, clings to the illusion that truth and virtue are possible in this world — until he can hold on no longer. He leads us to understand and resist the destructive force of stereotypes — until he himself runs afoul of them and instructs us as to their possible tragic truth. The stage for this drama is set at once. In the opening scene, set beneath an ominous full moon, in a peasant hut, Ma Dasan and his mistress, the widowed Yu'er, are making love. Dasan repeatedly tries to turn up the oil-lamp and begs to see her in the light while she firmly resists, when suddenly a knock on the door sends her scurrying from the bed to her usual hiding place. She is immediately revealed after all, not just to Dasan but to the film audience, naked front and rear [045]. Yet the one who knocks goes virtually unseen: a total stranger who answers only to the name of "*Wo*," or "Me," and who obliges Ma Dasan not to look — as Yu'er did, except now at gunpoint. "*Wo*" dumps two burlap bags on the earthen floor and, with hasty warnings to interrogate them and take good care of them until his return, he leaves [039]. Afterward he is envisioned only by the gun and the sword that he brandishes [046]. Easier to miss than to see is the mere one-half second (sixteen DVD frames) when Dasan briefly opens his

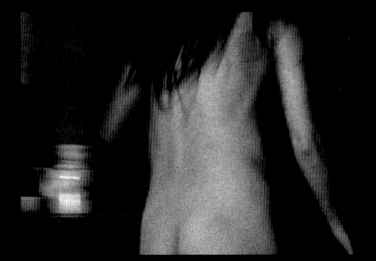

[045]

Yu'er exposed

[046]

[047]

"Wo" / "Me"

eyes and we glimpse "*Wo*" as a hooded phantom [047]. In time, if they haven't forgotten him altogether in the turmoil of events he has unleashed, the audience may come to speculate that this Beckett-like "Me" — unnamed, virtually unseen, and never to return to those who wait for him — represents the Communist presence in the film, but who knows? That mythic force will be far more distinguished through the course of the film by its absence than by its presence. The stereotype of the peace-loving, avoidant, fearful Chinese peasant is contrasted here with the image of the Communist agent — bold but secretive, forever working in the darkness. Soon afterwards, peasants and Communists will be triangulated with the Japanese, with nothing concealed about the forthright militancy of the Japanese and their disrespect for Chinese "cowardice."

How to dispose of living stereotypes, one not a translator, one not a samurai

When the two bags turn out to contain two prisoners [048] [049] captured in an ambush, bound and gagged, one a Japanese soldier and the other his Chinese translator, Dasan and the villagers are faced with the opportunity — with the vague yet obvious expectation — that they avenge themselves for Japan's brutal colonization. Yet Dasan would rather make love than war. He and his kind are heirs to two thousand years of self-contained village life and war brings nothing to them but conscription. This Chinese peasant village is wistfully named Rack-Armor Terrace and its villagers are steeped in submissive ways. In the midst of China's life-or-death struggle with Japanese colonizers, Ma Dasan becomes caught up in a philosophical tug-of-war with himself. Having survived the years of Japanese occupation with his historical neutrality intact, he is now disturbed in mere minutes by "*Wo*," trapped in a struggle between virtue and expedience. Dasan has two captives in his peasant hut, but he is as much their captive as they are his. Meeting to cope with the crisis, the village men propose many solutions of how to dispose of these enemies (without the Japanese finding out about it) — throttle them, bury them, behead them, just "run away and leave the sacks here" — but in the end, given Dasan's moral disposition and, especially, his dread fear that bringing death into the village will pollute his and Yu'er's unborn bastard child, it is the solutions and not the captives that are disposed of. Even after the task of dispatching them

[048]

[049]

[050]

[051]

Interrogation

falls to Dasan by lot, he hides them for months in a battlement of the Great Wall, that ineffective barrier which runs by this northerly village, keeping them alive through the winter with food and warm bedding that are in scarce supply. He attempts to hire two professional executioners, but both turn out to be frauds, perhaps as fearful and cowardly as he is. "We can't kill and we won't," confesses Yu'er. In the course of events, Dasan is exposed to all the stereotypes that purport to differentiate Chinese and Japanese behavior.

Devils is a study in demonization. But Ma Dasan rejects equally the demonizing of Chinese by Japanese and of Japanese by Chinese, and he clings instead to the values that bind people together as civilized human beings, as differentiated from mere animals. The film, however, has its own ideas about this and is structured around the pivotal question of whether Chinese and Japanese are different or the same, and it gives one answer after another: they're different, they're not different, they're different. In the end, however, every situation offers far greater complications than expected, and after virtually every permutation of every possible-seeming resolution has been explored, imagined, or put into practice, he is left with the realization that different men can aspire to entirely different values and that the differences can justify their behaving like dogs and asses toward each other. Civilization proves too thin, and Ma Dasan's crude efforts to harmonize himself with whatever comes his way, along with the twists and turns of fate visited upon him and the unmanageable flaws in his own character, all prove so damnably frustrating that by the end he has simply seen too much of real life, run out of options, and a quick death seems preferable to a lingering existence on this planet. His attempt to court reality and win it over gives way to a leap into fantasy — something of a reversal of *In the Heat of the Sun*.

It is the phantom "*Wo*, Me" who catalyzes the plot with a threat to destroy Dasan and the whole village if the prisoners are not interrogated by the time of his return to retrieve them. He never returns, which allows the problem of how to deal with the captives to linger throughout most of the film, but the interrogation he demanded begins apace [050] [051]. And with the interrogation, the flow of stereotypes begins. As the two bound prisoners pop out of their gunny sacks, much the worse for wear, they indeed look very much alike until the local villagers discover — to their surprise, and so much for appearances! — that one of them is a Chinese collaborator and that the two could not be more different. The Chinese prisoner "naturally" aspires to longevity and fears for his life, seeks security and practices inaction, survives to carry out his filial obligations. As the *Classic of Filial Piety*, the *Xiao jing*, admonishes,

> (A son) should not forget his parents in a single lifting up of his feet, and therefore he will walk in the highway and not take a bypath, he will use a boat and not attempt to wade through a stream; — not daring, with the body left him by his parents, to go in the way of peril.[104]

The Japanese prisoner fears only for his honor and struggles for a way to commit suicide rather than suffer the indignity and dishonor of imprisonment by enemy peasants.

Radically opposed Chinese and Japanese attitudes toward the body are fully played out here. The translator, Dong Hanchen, introduces himself to the villagers saying, "I turn Japanese into Chinese and Chinese into Japanese," but that is just what he doesn't do. Trying to protect the Japanese soldier, Hanaya Kosaburo, from his own Japaneseness, Dong Hanchen constantly mistranslates. The opening encounter reads something like this:

> Village head: *So, what's his name. Have him tell us himself.*
> Hanaya Kosaburo (in Japanese): *Shoot me! Kill me! If you've got the guts. Cowards!*
> Villagers: *How come his name's so long?*
> Village head: *Has he killed Chinese men? Violated Chinese women?*
> Hanaya (in Japanese): *Of course. That's what I came to China for.*
> Dong Hanchen ("translating" this): *He's new to China. Hasn't seen any women yet. He's killed no one. He's a cook.* Then to Hanaya: *Why are you doing this?*
> Hanaya: *I want to anger these cowards! I won't cooperate with swine!*
> Dong Hanchen (translating this): *He begs you not to kill him!*

"Translator" Dong Hanchen opens a humane channel of communications that offers some hope for a rapprochement between Chinese and Japanese, but it is predicated hopelessly on a deception. And Hanaya, even while bound hand and foot, proceeds in his attempts at suicide, repeatedly dashing his head against a wooden pillar.

This behavior, so mystifying to his Chinese captors, represents the modern revitalization of the medieval warrior ethic, described in Eiko Ikegami's account of such samurai rituals of violence as their "grim tradition" of beheading the enemy:

> Severing enemies' heads was an important custom of samurai warfare. During the medieval period, a major victory would always end with the piling up of dozens, even hundreds, of chopped-off heads in the commander's quarters.... The origins of the grim tradition are a mystery.... Whereas cutting off enemies' heads bestowed a significant honor on warriors, those who were defeated and decapitated were dishonored: an exchange of honor and dishonor.[105]

What a samurai feared for himself was not death and disfigurement but defeat and dishonor at the hand of the enemy, as Ikegami illustrates by a passage from *Heiji monogatari*: here, the samurai Takiguchi Toshitsune, wounded in battle, overhears his master command a vassal, "Don't let Takiguichi's head be taken by the enemy. Bring it to us," at which point Takiguchi extends his neck to the fellow samurai, saying, "That eases my mind."[106] Failing to bash his brains in, then tied up in padded blankets so that he can no longer keep trying, Hanaya decides to starve himself to death, takes Ma Dasan's generosity in trying to keep him alive as a form of Chinese cowardice, and spits his food in Ma Dasan's face when the peasant attempts to feed him:

> Hanaya: *Bastard! Humiliating an Imperial soldier! I'll kill you! Chinese pig!*
> Ma Dasan, to the translator: *What's he want?*
> Dong Hanchen: *White flour.*

When Ma Dasan and his mistress Yu'er, in a comedy of misunderstanding, proceed to go looking for white flour (possession of which was "hoarding," more than a mere luxury, and proscribed as a capital offense by the Japanese overlords), Hanaya takes this as an act of servility, as revolting to him as the his attempts at suicide are baffling to Dasan and the others. As Dasan's search for flour goes on, Hanaya continues the parade of stereotypes, saying: "Dong. Teach me some Chinese.... I want to swear at them. Infuriate them and they'll have to kill me. Chinese hate people who curse their ancestors.... I want to turn the curses you teach me into bullets to fire at them." When Dasan and his mistress return, Hanaya leers at them, sneers at them, and curses them [052] with the phrases Dong has taught him, which, in order to save Hanaya from himself, turn out to be, "Brother and sister-in-law, happy new year! You're my granddad, I'm your son." Yu'er looks at him [053], puzzled, and inquires, "The words are nice. Why does he sound so angry?" Ma Dasan, before correcting the genealogical inconsistency, replies with some stereotypes of his own: "Japs sound the same whether they're happy or angry. Why d'ya think we call them devils?" Hanaya, puzzled by the couple's tepid response to his intended insults, asks his translator, "Why aren't they angry?" to which Dong Hanchen explains, "Japanese are always cursing them. They're used to it."

The flow of stereotypes and invectives is unceasing. The captives are certain that their white-flour dumplings are a "last meal" and so they must be at death's door. But now it is Hanaya's turn to be puzzled. "Why don't they act like they're going to kill us?" he asks. A despondent Dong Hanchen begins to toy cynically with the stereotypes that have been so handily passed around: "Even when a Chinese kills someone, his expression never changes." As it begins to dawn on them that they aren't really going to die and instead are the recipients of an inexplicable generosity, the Chinese interpreter is naturally relieved, but Hanaya, his death deferred once more, begins to cry bitterly. "What now?" the village head asks. The revitalized interpreter again replies gratuitously, "The Japs are like this. They love to cry. They love to sing."

But stereotypes are made to be broken — one of them, that only the Japanese soldier, and not the Chinese, would have learned to choose death over captivity is itself a stereotype without much weight in either fiction or reality[107] — and throughout much of the film, tragedy is forestalled by this kind of comedy, as Jiang Wen repeatedly plays with and deconstructs such ethnic clichés only to have his characters resurrect them all over again in new forms and contexts.[108] When Hanaya finally discovers that Dong Hanchen has tricked him with phrases he has been taught, he's struck painfully by the fact that this lowly Chinese is smarter than he is and spurts out "Educated people are so evil. I hate you educated people." And Dong, the clever translator, grasping through this verbal shift a degrading of Hanaya's authority, shouts back, "I hate stupid Japanese like you! Lowlife peasant! No fucking dignity at all."

[052]

Hanaya: "Brother and Sister-in-law"

[053]

Yu'er: "Why does he sound so angry?"

Late in the narrative, as the captives avoid one encounter with death after another, it spills out that this spitting, sputtering, scruffy-looking Hanaya is just what he looks like: not a modern samurai at all but just a lowly foot soldier ("My parents raise silkworms! Not samurai!"), another peasant just like his captors, both humiliated and overwhelmed by the fact that the peasants gave their own starvation rations to keep him alive for a half year, that the widow personally dressed his wounds. Hanaya was just trying to live up to the standards of his own culture and of his troop commander, a true samurai and childhood friend who rose out of the same village. A visible realignment takes place, Hanaya identifying now in a transnational way with his fellow peasants and plotting with them to get himself and his interpreter exchanged as hostages in return for two cartloads of grain for the villagers; in the end, they get six cartloads, one for each month of sustaining the captives. While this might be interpreted as humanism triumphant, it might equally well be seen as fraternization with the enemy and collaboration.

To touch a samurai, to mount his horse

After Hanaya is returned to his regiment, the audience is introduced to the real Japanese thing: a clean-cut, athletic, totally alert, coolly disciplined fighting machine, troop captain Sakatsuka Inokichi [054]. This twentieth-century samurai honors Hanaya's deal with the Chinese peasants because in his words, "Unlike the Chinese, the Japanese are honorable people." But he proceeds to beat Hanaya mercilessly, having long ago reported him dead and installed as a martyr at the Yasukuni Jinja, the shrine for Japan's fallen warriors — a modern flashpoint point of antagonism between Japan and China, as director Jiang Wen and most of his Chinese audience are well aware.[109] Hanaya now has a new reason to commit suicide, if his commander doesn't kill him first. And Sakatsuka will take further revenge as well for this drain on his goodwill.

The contrast between Sakatsuka (tautly drawn, reserved, purposeful, and totally confident) and Ma Dasan [055] (big but flabby, morally inquisitive but usually uncertain, highly emotional and frequently clueless) is visible in every detail of their appearance and their behavior. Ma Dasan, a man of many faces, is an inhabitant of the world of comedy, a master of improvisation, an alcoholic character, essentially, but with no need for drink to achieve that effect.

98

Ma Dasan

He is, by theatrical type, a background figure designed for the brief relief of dramatic tension, but here he is cast in the foreground, pitched uncomprehending into the midst of tragedy; a type intended, elsewhere, to provide the audience with emotional distance and intellectual perspective, a safe remove from harsh reality, he is here obliged to defend that distance, and then, failing to do so, he is destined to lose that perspective himself and to contribute doubly to the audience's own confusion about his role and its meaning. Sakatsuka, a tight-jawed man, as clear-minded as Dasan is beclouded, can scarcely laugh and then only at the foibles and weaknesses of the Chinese peasantry, each smile but a smirk. The difference between them is not, in itself, problematic but rather emblematic of the two countries. But to Sakatsuka, the kidnapped Hanaya's survival and dalliance with the enemy represents an intolerable blurring of the moral distinctions between the ruling Japanese and their degenerate subjects. As Hanaya makes his unwelcome return to ranks, even the commander's horse (wearing the imperial Rising Sun upon her forehead) lowers her head for shame [056]. Immediately, Hanaya's fraternizing with the enemy — this reverse assimilation of guard with prisoner, this cultural miscegenation — is paralleled by a startling event: the villager's donkey comes happily bounding into the military compound and proceeds to molest the Japanese captain's mare [057] [058], without the slightest respect for superior breed![110] Even the Japanese commander cannot help but smile, ever so slightly [059], but this event hovers ominously and alarmingly over the whole outcome of the film — a turning point, as that smile, that smirk, turns slowly to a smoldering rage [060] that one knows must sooner or later flare up into a full blaze.

In time, the fraternization is resumed — abetted, ironically, by commander Sakatsuka, who regards his troops, withdrawn from the noble field of battle, as morally weakened by the unmanly task of occupation. The date is August 15, 1945. Japan has surrendered, but only he knows that. (The Western viewing audience, unless they know this date by heart, will not realize this fact until later). Militant to the core, but now feeling betrayed by his own emperor, and more loyal to the culture of battle than to his government, he invites the entire village to a nighttime fete with his troops to celebrate their clever trade of captives for cartloads of grain. The two sides exchange songs, and as the alcohol flows freely, the Chinese villagers behave increasingly equal to their military

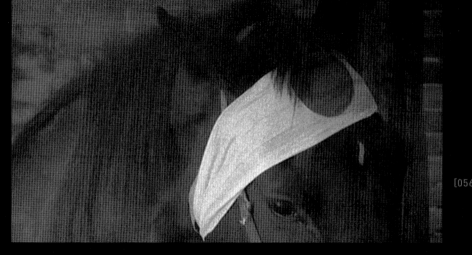

[056]

Embarrassed horse

[057]

[058]

Sakatsuka smirks

[059]

[060]

Sakatsuka enraged

Touching Sakatsuka

[061]

[062]

Hanaya cringes

masters. Sakatsuka takes it all in patiently, tempting them on, biding his time: surely, the audience must wonder, to what end? One of the villagers accuses the commander of being fearful since he is so dependent on his weapons, and forgetting his assigned, lowly place, he repeatedly touches Sakatsuka, patting him on the shoulder, then rubbing the top of his head [061] — just as the villagers' donkey "touched" the commander's horse. Sakatsuka smiles an evil smile, and those who see it cringe [062] — the audience must cringe, too — and then the smoldering rage flares up. Having warned his troops against pollution by proximity, having witnessed its degrading effects on others and now experienced it himself, there is now nothing left but to eliminate the polluters.

The time to reassert proper military order has come, the troops are mobilized to the task, and the entire community is slaughtered, including widow Yu'er's young son, Little Thresher (see frame 040). Carried out by a firelight that blazes like the satanic fires of a bombed-out Tokyo or a nuclear hell, the vengeful massacre is horrific, and none of the aesthetic sensibilities of the audience are spared. Sakatsuka commands, demonic. Swords thrust frontally into bodies penetrate the back side. Hard to withdraw, they are slowly and carefully cleaned of gore before being put to bloody use again. One man is thrown down the well, which is then filled with the ransom grain. The village elder is thrown live onto the bonfire. The pregnant Yu'er and father-to-be Dasan, returning late to the "celebration," witness from afar the whole village set ablaze and are the only ones spared. Dasan survives only to face an empty future. The cruel spectacle is played out before our eyes to the authentic tones of Hirohito's famed radio broadcast, describing "a new, cruel bomb" and asserting, ironically, that "Should we continue the fight, not only would the Japanese nation be obliterated, but human civilization would be extinguished."

The human beast, corporal punishment, and the spectacle of it all

The war ended, the Chinese military arrives in the county town to round up Japanese troops and establish a new political order within the community. To establish his authority there, the Nationalist major uses the collaborator Dong Hanchen as a model victim and has him shot (see frames 041–044). Ma Dasan, having struggled and sacrificed to protect Dong Hanchen, having strained to remain above the partisan fray, only to watch his village razed and his community destroyed by Japanese troops as the direct result of his efforts, now joins the crowd who witness the spectacle of Hanchen being shot by his fellow Chinese countrymen while the Japanese troops — invaders and butchers — are pardoned and prepared to be repatriated.

Early in the film, a pair of unruly Japanese soldiers with nothing better to do than stir up more than the usual trouble begin trying to trap Dasan's chickens for a lunchtime snack, while Dasan and Yu'er try desperately to conceal the secret of their prisoners hidden just a few feet away. Now, his village wiped out, and having watched all hope for social justice blasted with the public execution of Hanchen, Dasan is trying to scrape through by selling cigarettes when the same two soldiers show up to buy some. Dasan goes berserk, slaying the two and following it up with a vengeful slaughter of unarmed Japanese prisoners. With Sakatsuka as his prime target, he leaves a trail of savaged bodies that parallels the Japanese slaughter of his fellow villagers. He ends up wounding Sakatsuka only slightly and so ultimately falls short. *Devils on the Doorstep* began with, then demolished, then again built up stereotypes of Chinese-Japanese difference; here, difference finally collapses, once and for all, as Ma Dasan — like commander Sakatsuka and the other Japanese — ends up putting his own considerations ahead of the lives of others. Finally subdued, Ma Dasan is condemned to be decapitated.

Such acts of vengeance, in fact, were rare and were strictly prohibited by the American military command, which was in charge of policy in China at the time of the turnover from Japanese to Nationalist control.[111] But enforcement here is carried out by the Chinese, a cinematic demonstration that while the Chinese had proved largely ineffectual against the enemy, they are still effective at devouring their own, as in short-story writer Lu Xun's celebrated critique of Chinese "cannibalism."[112] First Hanchen and now Dasan fall prey to Chinese justice. The rationale for terminating Ma Dasan is lodged in a public speech by the Nationalist Major Gao [063]:

> *Perhaps some will say Ma Dasan only killed "Jap devils" and call it "resistance."*
> *But what is "resistance"? Battles fought with Japanese troops, the struggle*
> *against invasion, those are acts of resistance. But Ma Dasan's wanton slaughter*

[063]

Major Gao and the GIs

of POWs who had lost the will to resist was a false resistance. Perhaps some will argue that such profound hatred was the result of Japanese atrocities. Who of our 400 million compatriots doesn't hate the Japanese? My own parents were killed by Japanese bombs. My left leg [which he then slaps, so that he almost falls over and has to be propped back up by American GIs] was shattered in the final battle. Who could be more motivated to kill former Japanese soldiers? Who has the best reason for revenge? Me. Major Gao. And who is the most constrained from such action? Me. Major Gao. Because I am a soldier, I must follow orders.

This condemnation of Ma Dasan's actions, and therefore of Dasan himself, may seem straightforward enough, and perhaps it is sufficient to the film's purpose to show that even an admirable and well-intentioned character like Ma Dasan can be pushed by the force of events beyond the limits of acceptable moral behavior. But one suspects that it takes more of a rationale than this to justify the demise of a carefully developed film "hero" and that this explanation is just too simple, or at least incomplete. In fact, what Jiang Wen is illustrating here is nothing less than the reversion of decision-making authority, in matters of social justice, from the people (where it had resided in the absence of central Chinese command during the chaotic wartime years, as seen in the communal decision making processes of Ma Dasan's Rack-Armor Terrace) to the state, and the reassertion by the state of its exclusive right to the exercise and control of violence in peacetime (or put negatively, the authority to demonize and terrorize to maintain its authority), which it had been forced to share in wartime. Located here in a Nationalist context, this same assertion of exclusive state authority over life-and-death justice could just as readily be projected backward onto the successive dynasties through the whole length of the imperial era or forward into the era of Communist rule. The Nationalists, here, are ciphers for the centralization and unchanging harshness of Chinese justice, past, present, and future.

As the executioner prepares his sword for Dasan's neck, a solitary donkey wanders about in the background, pausing to look right into the camera (see frame 069). Easily overlooked, taken as quirky techniques of cinematic pacing, or dismissed as mere bits of quaint rusticity, this and numerous other visual links of man to beast are examples of the filmmakers' telling use of visual detail, not just on the execution ground but throughout a film in which humans are slaughtered like animals. In fact, this species-transference is part of a steady stream supplied by the film, verbal and visual, both anthropomorphic (the Japanese commander's horse bowing its head in shame at Hanaya's return, and in turn being shamed by a Chinese donkey) (see frames 056–058) and zoomorphic (the constant Japanese reference to the Chinese as pigs and dogs — Hanaya: "I won't cooperate with swine!" and "Mongrels can't even shoot straight"; Dong Hanchen, in an uppity moment, to Hanaya: "You don't get it, do you, pig brain?").

The film itself, ironically, indulges in its own satirical species-confusion. In the early scene in which the pair of Japanese soldiers attempt to supplement their diet by commandeering Dasan's chickens, a minor episode both menacing and comic that has its unexpectedly major impact on the outcome of the narrative, the fearful peasants go running about the courtyard as terrified as the chickens themselves, while the soldiers scurry after them shouting "halt" to the chickens and the Chinese alike; just in case the pursuers come too close to the captives hidden indoors, Dasan prepares to strike, positioning himself like a roosting chicken ready to peck at the hand that reaches to seize its eggs and arming himself for the possibility with a cleaver used to slaughter fowl. Late in the film, as surrendering Japanese troops are herded into the city square, they are set side by side with a flock of sheep, the two groups juxtaposed for comparison purposes, equally docile and mindless, implying that the Japanese were no less a herd of sheep when brutally bleating their *banzais* to the emperor than they are now in submitting, at their emperor's command, to the militarily incompetent Chinese [064]. Major Gao makes a serious attempt to place the Nationalists' newly established military authority on high moral ground (conspicuously propped up by swaggering Americans at his side), even as he begins to carry out the same harsh measures against his own fellow citizens as the Japanese had before him. But in another animal moment, this effort is interrupted by a marauding pig which suddenly enters, squealing wildly and riding off with a startled Nationalist soldier on his back [065]; it is like a diagetic Bronx cheer unleashed by the film director and makes a laughing stock of the Chinese major among the delighted villagers, who all squeal as loudly as the pig.

[064]

Sheep

[066]

Donkey kick

Most importantly, the parallel drawn between the villagers' lowly donkey outrageously miscegenating with troop commander Sakatsuka's noble steed on the one hand, and, on the other, the Chinese peasant daring to address Sakatsuka as an equal, to accuse him of weakness, to touch him on the shoulder, then place his hand on Sakatsuka's head (see frame 061), illuminates the boundary between master and slave that both are obliged to rigorously observe, and defines an ultimate taboo; crossing that boundary is rebellion, an assault on the superior civilization, that must be ruthlessly suppressed.

And most sadly, just as Dasan is prepared for his death not by Japanese "devils" but by his fellow countrymen, with Major Gao asking "Who has the best reason for revenge?", the narrative thrust is interrupted by the cinematic insertion of another animal analog, an irritated mother donkey digging a sudden sharp kick of the hoof into the side of her startled, innocently nursing foal [066].[113]

Failing in his violence even as he did in his efforts to avoid violence, the captured Dasan becomes to all others nothing more than a barnyard beast, defined as such both by the newly established Chinese rulers and by the camera itself. "What distinguishes a man from a beast?" asks the Nationalist major who passes sentence on him. "You don't deserve to be called Chinese. You don't even deserve to be called human. How can a Chinese soldier sully his hands with the blood of such scum?" As a final agonizing twist, based on old, unchanging values, the major insists that this task be carried out by Japanese because, as Dasan has lowered himself to the status of an animal, his blood shouldn't pollute the hands of a Chinese soldier. The Japanese soldier to whom the task of taking Dasan's head devolves is none other than Hanaya, who helped get Dasan into this cycle of events in the first place and whose life Dasan repeatedly risked his own to spare [067]. In the course of the tale, Hanaya was "corrupted" by his lengthy contact with the Chinese "animals." "You've been with them for too long. You're getting too close to them," is how Sakatsuka describes a fellow soldier's decline, the greatest risk run by an occupying force. Now, ironically, in the service of "justice," by taking on a task regarded by the Chinese as beneath their dignity, Hanaya is given the opportunity to recover his Japanese dignity. The elaborate Japanese ritual by which Hanaya's feat of swordsmanship is carefully carried out is observed by Gu Changwei's camera with equal care. At the last minute, as the sword is about

[067]

Dasan and executioner Hanaya

[068]

to swing, the swordsman pauses to flick away a solitary ant that crawls across the back of Dasan's neck [068], sparing the ant,[114] preserving the "purity" of the ceremony (which is more important than the life of Dasan himself), and allowing Dasan, impatient for it all to be over, to deliver the ungrateful Hanaya a final unforgiving glare. Then Hanaya butchers "the beast."

Chinese personification of the animal realm, anthropomorphism, in both positive and negative terms, is a topic vast enough to fill many a book. The horse, for example, was a universally known metaphor for the government servant, strong and docile.[115] A single look at the eye of a well-painted horse (fig. 26), rendered with a strictly human, most unhorselike, expressively raised eyebrow and exaggerated, reddened tear duct while the remainder of the horse is otherwise executed in remarkably accurate detail, is enough to suggest that the painting is less about animal (cf. fig. 27 and frame 056) than man — in this painting's case, with an accompanying inscription by the fourteenth-century scholar-painter himself detailing the political self-defense that the image presents.[116] A reverse equation of man with beast — man *as* beast, zoomorphism — is found in Fan Kuai's famous third-century BCE admonition to the imperial pretender Xiang Yu about why in his own faltering behavior he had better avoid the precedent of China's recently deceased First Emperor, whose short-lived dynasty vanished almost as soon as he did: "The King of Qin had the heart of a tiger and a wolf. He killed men as though he could never finish, he punished men as though he were afraid he would never get around to

Figure 26 Ren Renfa, *Two Horses, Fat and Lean*, ink and colors on silk, detail of a handscroll, early 14th century. Palace Museum, Beijing. Photograph: James Cahill.

Figure 27 Unidentified photographer, the race horse Secretariat, c. 1975.

them all, and the whole world revolted against him."[117] This same epithet, "You've got the heart of a wolf," is hurled at Hanaya by a Chinese villager as his betrayal becomes evident at the outset of the massacre.

The relationship of humans to the animals, historically, is directly linked to Chinese concepts of justice and punishment. There is a great deal written about the so-called five punishments (*wu xing*) in classical Chinese literature, from the *Shu jing* and the *Analects* down through the *Book of Filial Piety*, and in the dynastic codes of law from Qin to Qing. Various enumerations of the "five" at different times included branding the forehead, cutting off the nose or feet, strangulation, decapitation, drawing and quartering, cutting out the ribs of the still-living victim, and boiling in cauldrons of oil,[118] which makes these means by which "civilization" was enforced seem particularly uncivilized by modern standards.[119] Directed against some three thousand different possible offenses, according to Confucius, the five punishments more than anything else are leveled against breaches of filial piety, that fundamental virtue without which there would be, in his words, "nothing lofty…no law…no relationships," in other words, no civilization and no species.[120]

As Chinese concepts of justice would have it, in intentionally violating the official order of things one offends against civilization itself, abandons one's humanity, becomes no more than a "barbarian" and deserves no more mercy than an animal, for whom the Chinese have traditionally had little empathy. Many of China's minority peoples and surrounding "uncivilized" tribes had names which were written by characters using the dog-radical (the Xianyun and Di tribes of the north, the Quan-Rong of the northwestern highlands, the Hui Muslims of the west) or the sheep/goat-radical (the Qiang or Jiang-Rong of the northwestern highlands), or the insect-radical (the Man tribes of the south). This usage varied: under Manchu rule, these radicals were sometimes omitted, and the practice was largely eliminated after 1949, probably for reasons of simplification and standardization, with a few exceptions, like the character for Jews, still written with the dog-radical. "But none of these generics," writes Endymion Wilkinson,

> have influenced the Chinese language as much as *hu* (the basic meaning
> is dewlap; hence beard; hence the bearded ones; hence barbarians; hence

foreigners). A memory of the strange (barbarous) ways in which the non-Han spoke is reflected in the many expressions beginning with *hu* such as *huche* (talk nonsense), *hushuo* (drivel), or *hushuo badao* (talk rubbish). In addition, the memory of the barbarian's uncouth behavior is recalled in terms such as *huchi husai* (eat anything and everything), *huchou* (body [armpit] odor), or *hugao* (be promiscuous; mess things up).[121]

"Derogatory terms for naming the barbarians were also common," Wilkinson continues:

> The usual practice was to use words such as slave (*nu*), devil (*gui*), caitiff (*lu*), or robber (*zei*) linked to the old generic terms *hu*, *yi*, *man*, and *fan*. Thus the chief enemy of the Qin and Han empires, the Xiongnu, were called *Nuxin* [slave-hearted or slave-brained].... Facial features, such as the length of the nose, skin color, the color of the eyes, hair styles, hirsuteness, the size of the body, or just general appearance were also used to nickname non-Han peoples."[122]

In myth and image, this persistent tradition took form in the "documentary" record as illustrated maps, illustrated texts, and encyclopedias, and could readily be applied to any ethnically alien enemy of the moment. Such were the barbarians (fig. 28) from the western reaches of the Wusun Kingdom in the third century BCE, three-clawed creatures covered with long hair, whose leaders, not surprisingly, oppressed their own common people.[123] The Japanese, historically, were known in China as the Wa people, or dwarfs.

As an occasional theme in Chinese painting, *Clearing Out a Mountain Forest* (*Sou shan tu*; sometimes entitled *Searching for Demons on Mt. Guankou*) (fig. 29) is unusual for its display of violence and a troubled relationship between man and beast.[124] With narrative and geographical reference to the rechanneling of Sichuan's rivers by the famed hydrologist Li Bing of the third century BCE and forest-clearing by his son Erlang, later deified by Daoists as protective divinities, the theme has historical roots in the bringing of north Chinese culture south under the auspices of the predynastic Qin state. Like comic book characters illustrating the adage that it takes a demon to vanquish a demon, the grotesque characters in this painting are hybrid beasts engaged in helping

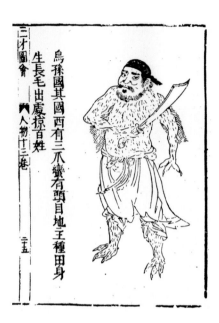

Figure 28 Three-clawed barbarian from the Wusun Kingdom. From Wang Qi, ed., *Sancai tuhui*, *renwu*, *juan* 13, 25.

Figure 29 Anonymous (15th century), *Searching for Demons on Mount Guankou* (*Guankou sou shan tu*). Handscroll, ink on silk; painting: 48.4 × 935.9 cm; frontispiece: 49.7 × 117.0 cm; colophons: 48.7 × 98.3 cm. Princeton University Art Museum, Gift of John B. Elliott, Class of 1951 (y1982-97).

to vanquish others who appear as female lovelies but whose long courtly robes subtly disclose hideous monkeylike feet or birdlike talons. Beyond the removal of some vaguely fearsome arboreal spirits, *Clearing Out a Mountain Forest* seems to document the demonization of China's "uncivilized" neighbors and the wholesale vanquishing of aboriginal inhabitants from these forested lands, making way for agrarian civilization, and commemorates this as one of the civic responsibilities of early rulership.[125]

This bestialization of "peripheral" peoples reinforced the leading roles of those in traditional positions of authority, as recounted by Richard von Glahn:

> The native peoples of the south, chiefly hill tribes alien to the culture of the Yellow River valley, appeared no less bestial and savage than the land they inhabited. Indeed, in Chinese eyes, the "barbaric" peoples of the south were kindred to the demonic spirits that lurked among them. Throughout the Era of Disunion, and even long after, the forested mountains of the south evoked images of demonic creatures like the *shanxiao*, ever ready to prey upon interlopers from the civilized world.... Since at least the early Zhou period, Chinese perceived the world as an arena of relentless struggle between civilization and barbarism. The enlightened monarch, anointed by Heaven, used his authority to fashion a world of symmetry, regularity, and tranquility. But this ideal state was perpetually besieged by the entropic forces of disorder.... The mythologies that coalesced around the figures of ancient sage-kings during the Warring States period depicted them as civilizers who tamed the hostile wilderness and its terrifying creatures. These myths accentuated the "panoptic gaze of the sage-ruler," to use Robert Campany's apt phrase: through tours of inspection and collection of tribute, the ruler acquired knowledge of the peoples and territories on the periphery of his realm and used it to fix them in their proper places within the orbit of imperial control.[126]

China gradually became more familiar with and more realistic about its Asian neighbors only to encounter a more distant and stranger group of barbarians, Europeans covered with body hair. Ironically, the new barbarians would develop theories on evolutionary development that reinforced older Chinese popular notions linking humans to animals in a developmental chain, associating such features as hairiness with primitives at the lower end of the developmental order.[127]

> Racial discourse was a dominant practice which cut across most political positions, from the fascist core of the Guomindang to the communist theories of Li Dazhao. Its fundamental role in the construction of racialised boundaries between Self and Other, its powerful appeal to a cultural sense of belonging based on presumed immutable links of blood, its authoritative worldview in which social differences could be explained in terms of stable biological laws, all these aspects provided racial discourse with a singular resilience: it shaped the identity of millions of people in Republican China, as it had done for people in Europe and the United States.[128]

Membership in the "Yellow race," as descendents of the Yellow Emperor, was embraced by modern Chinese as a source of pride. Chinese textbooks taught that:

> Mankind is divided into five races. The yellow and white races are relatively strong and intelligent. Because the other races are feeble and stupid, they are being exterminated by the white race. Only the yellow race competes with the white race. This is so-called evolution."[129]

The political reformer Kang Youwei (1858–1927) wrote of Africans "with their iron faces, silver teeth, slanting jaws like a pig, front view like an ox, full breasts and long hair, their hands and feet dark black, stupid like sheep or swine," an attitude that remains all too pervasive in China even now.[130] "To this day ... the Cantonese describe the Tanka, a population group of boat-dwellers in South China, as people with six toes on each foot; they are claimed to be of non-Han descent. The small toenails of the Mongols are said by the Han to be cloven, while minorities in Hainan have long been alleged to have a tail."[131]

Such animalism, in all of its forms, cheapens human life and paves the way for the easy acceptance of injustice. Clinical experiments have shown how readily and severely even the most minimal labeling of people in bestial terms leads to increased harshness toward them by others in a position to deliver punishment.[132] A study of violence and punishment during the Cultural Rev-olution, when victims were often herded and squeezed into intolerably small "ox pens" (*niu peng*), recounts that,

> From childhood they had been taught that landlords, reactionaries, counter-revolutionaries, rightists, bad elements, ox ghosts and snake spirits, traitors, spies, and a whole host of class enemies were less than human, legitimate objects of violent attack. Recalling how one of his students participated in beating to death a colleague during the Cultural Revolution, an elderly pro-fessor remarked, "I can almost understand how it happened. The landlords were the enemies then. They weren't people, really. You could use violence against them. It was acceptable."[133]

What is acceptable to the culture and unacceptable in the film is the reduc-tion of Ma Dasan's tragedy to an occasion for public spectacle, by modern standards robbing this civil ceremony of the last shreds of civilizing value. No sympathy comes from the Chinese villagers, who laugh and howl and who have yet to claim a better world for themselves than the one that their Japa-nese overlords left them with. In this, *Devils on the Doorstep* joins a lonely tra-dition embraced by Lu Xun, whose medical studies ended and political writing career began in 1906 upon seeing just such a beheading of a Chinese pris-oner by a Japanese official, Lu Xun being distressed most of all by the lack of sympathetic response by the Chinese *who looked on*.[134] The loss of a head suggests, more than the loss of life, the loss of reason, and does not concern the rationality of the victim so much as it does that of the perpetrators and the compliant (perhaps jubilant) witnesses to the event. As one scholar puts it, "Enter the back door of rationality, and one finds a bloodthirsty impulse being enacted.... Lu Xun simply concludes that Confucianism functions as the perpetrator and protector of institutionalized savagery."[135]

Historically enshrined, Lu Xun's critique of Chinese "cannibalism" con-tinues as a living tradition in literature and the visual arts to this day. The contemporary artist Zhi Lin has created five monumental, twelve-foot-tall compositions entitled *Five Capital Executions in China* (e.g., fig. 30), researched and painted over an eleven-year period from 1993 to 2003.[136] In each of Zhi Lin's works, the populace incorporate the extermination of prisoners into their daily rounds and public entertainments, approaching the public spectacle with moods ranging from pleasure to wariness to indifference: feasting colorfully among the starving, watching an auspicious dragon dance during a drawing-and-quartering execution, calmly watching a beheading from the vantage of a butcher's market. As in Zhi Lin's works, just like a well-attended Southern lynching, the children present in *Devils on the Doorstep* learn to laugh and skip and jump about without being disturbed by the central presence of brutality,

Figure 30 Zhi Lin (b. 1959), *Drawing and Quartering*, from the series *Five Capital Executions in China*, 2002. Hanging scroll mounted as a *thangka*; charcoal on canvas with screen printing on ribbons. Drawing: 106 × 74 in. (image), 144 × 84 in. (mounting). Princeton University Art Museum, Museum purchase, Fowler McCormick, Class of 1921, Fund, with gifts from the P.Y. and Kinmay W. Tang Center for East Asian Art, Alisan Fine Arts, Ltd.—Alice King Gallery, and Thaw Charitable Trust (2005-131). Photo: Bruce M. White.

Figure 31 Artist unknown, "Darwin's Theory Illustrated — The Creation of Chinaman and Pig," cartoon from *The Wasp*, January 6, 1877. From Philip P. Choy et al., eds., *The Coming Man: 19th-Century American Perceptions of the Chinese*, pl. 75.

Figure 32 Chen Chieh-jen, *Revolt in the Soul and Body: The Image of Identical Twins*, black-and-white photograph, 1998. From Petr Nedoma and Chang Tsong-zung, *A Strange Heaven: Contemporary Chinese Photography*, 33.

everyone here behaving with a civility that divorces them from the plight of the victims and robs *the public* of its humanity.[137] Not stopping to question which ones among themselves might someday become victims (painter Zhi Lin includes self-portraits as both victim and witness), they participate from their earliest years in a subtle process of normalization of the regimen that perpetuates the regime. The many details of these works are historically derived but interspersed in terms of time and place to assure the universality of the critique. Accordingly, Zhi Lin's current work responds to the racialization of Chinese railway workers in nineteenth-century America, where bestial imagery — popular cartoons of Chinese as rats and pigs (fig. 31) — was all too common.[138]

Just as with the original staging of such historical scenes and situations, each recording and rerecording of them involves a further violation of the victim's dignity, a re-victimization. The Taiwanese photographer Chen Chieh-jen, who similarly transports himself into the historical context by digitally manipulating original photographs (fig. 32), writes that

> As we critique the history of the photographic image, we remember that photography came to the world's 'peripheries' along with colonialism. Peripheral peoples and societies were the photographed, serving as the viewed, the narrated and the silent in photographic history…. Just as peripheral peoples feared the camera had the power to take their souls, in today's society, where media controls the world, the image has become a tool of domination over man, and people come closer and closer to having their souls extracted by the image.[139]

At the conclusion of *Devils on the Doorstep*, the noble but naive Ma Dasan — Jiang Wen's cinematic victim, peripheralized, bestialized — is about to have his soul extracted and the two viewing audiences (those on the screen watching and those watching the screen) are about to become party to that extraction. Dasan has now wandered into an ambivalent, interrogatory, and untenable "third space" somewhere between the native passivity of China's peasantry and the uniformly militant, unquestioning, and equally unforgiving codes of the Japanese imperialists, the Chinese Nationalists, and the Communists. Reduced to bestial status and to animal behavior, when allowed to make a final statement before his decapitation, Dasan begins to bray like an inarticulate donkey [069].

In the modern classic *Lord of the Flies* (whose "lord" is a satanical boar's head, a beast of the innermost imagination around which the insects of the title buzz), the finest character is a young boy progressively identified with a wild pig and hunted down by his own child comrades. William Golding's novel

[069]

Dasan brays

ascribes society's penchant for violence not to race or racism, not to national-
ism or politics, but rather to what Golding himself referred to as "the defects
of human nature."[140] *Devils'* target, likewise, knows no age or nation. Director
Jiang Wen states,

> I went to Japan for the first time in 1991, and visited the Yasukuni Shrine.
> Nearly everything I saw there reminded me of China — the shrine could have
> been Chinese. Since then, I've visited Japan many times and I've come to
> realize that there aren't two types of person and that war crimes are not
> fundamentally a Chinese-Japanese issue. The real issue is war itself. It's
> war that changes people. In any war, there are the strong and the weak.
> And what nourishes war is not necessarily the strength of one side; it could
> equally be the weakness of the other. There's an inter-dependency in play.
> It's almost like a yin-yang phenomenon.[141]

Like *The Lord of the Flies*, *Devils* focuses on "the beast," the devils in man,
inbred and waiting to be unleashed. And like the novel, the film subtly embroi-
ders its tale, embodies its message, and enriches its imagery with the inter-
play of men and animals.

Who wasn't there and who was

When the Chinese military arrives in the county town, they are led by Major
Gao. He, in turn, is escorted (and one might say led) by a pair of jeep-driving,
gum-chewing American bodyguards (see frame 063). Here are the liberators,
and they are not the Communists of mythic lore, who remain as invisible as
the hooded "*Wo*, Me." "*Wo*," who may or may not have been a cadre, started
this narrative chain, but he disappeared from view without helping to guide it
away from its course toward disaster — a metaphor too grand to ignore.

There is no affinity, here or elsewhere in the film, between villagers and
cadres because there are no cadres. Street musicians are toadies who sing
the praise of whoever rules. Once they chanted, "Welcome the Japanese to the
neighborhood. / Eight hundred years ago we were all of one brood. / We all write
with characters, and when they beat us it really tickles…. / We love the Imperial
Army like family…." Now they proclaim, "China, UK, US, USSR, together no one
beats us." Communist anti-Japanese resistance has no existence. Even here,

what authority would the Chinese authorities have without American power to back them up? To watch *Devils on the Doorstep* is to witness a different history than that described in Chinese textbooks. Here, the audience hears of the American bomb that brought things to a sudden halt, watches meathead American troops who chew their huge wads of gum and blink their heavily lidded eyes in well-rehearsed comic unison—looking dumb but tough and in control—and one sees the town festooned with banners not of Marx, Engels, Lenin, and Mao but of Roosevelt and Churchill, Stalin and Chiang Kai-shek [070], a parody of things to come. It is not a scene to please the Chinese censor.

Various reasons have been given for why this film was banned by Chinese authorities and its director suspended indefinitely from future directing of films: its unauthorized submission to the Cannes festival competition, for one (and the one most commonly suggested); for another, the lack of hostility displayed by the Chinese (especially Dasan and Yu'er) toward the Japanese invaders, displacing the Chinese epic tale of anti-Japanese resistance by this folktale of fraternization with the enemy (who, in turn, often turn out to be more like clowns than monsters—taken by some as an historical insult to the memory of the many Chinese who suffered and died so horribly);[142] yet another: strictly bureaucratics.[143] One rarely knows for sure the precise reasoning of China's film censors, and all of these are plausible factors, though they are speculation at best and the film authorities' real thoughts will probably never be known. "I've asked seven times for a meeting with Film Bureau officials," Jiang Wen himself has claimed, "but with no success."[144]

Still, one more potent rationale for the censors' extreme response to *Devils on the Doorstep*, not mentioned elsewhere, could be attached here, not anything that was shown in the film but rather that which was not: who *wasn't* there when the war was won. Just think about "Me, *Wo*." Think, too, of who was not there to resist the reinstallation of Nationalist authority. Peter Hessler gives this account:

> The ban [on Jiang Wen] was never officially proclaimed, although two mysterious documents were leaked to Web sites. Supposedly, they had come from the Film Bureau. One was entitled "Propaganda Briefing No. 28," and it noted that the government was "suspending Jiang Wen for all film- and

[070]

Allied leaders

TV-related activities inside China." ... The second leaked document — "Comments from the Film Censorship Committee" — identified twenty specific places in which Jiang Wen had changed his script without permission. The sex scene was inappropriate: "The strong imagery and explicit sound stimulates the sensory organs in a vulgar manner." The committee also complained about the end of the film, which showed the Kuomintang controlling postwar China without resistance from the villagers: "It severely distorts the history. It doesn't achieve the goal of criticizing and sneering at the KMT." But the biggest problem was the passivity of the film's Chinese villagers. The document noted that one scene portrayed them giving good food to the Japanese prisoner and the Chinese collaborator: "Objectively it shows that even during times of war, under such difficult living conditions, the Chinese civilians do not hate the Japanese invaders, on the contrary, they try their best to satisfy the prisoners' needs.... This violates history severely."[145]

One of those Hessler interviewed, a young boy of twelve from the village near Panjiakou Reservoir, Hebei province, where most of the filming took place, got it right: "The peasants didn't resist. There was no Red Army, no Workers' Army, no guerillas — none of them showed up. That's the problem with the movie."[146]

The narrative of *Devils* and the absence or near-absence of Communist cadres from it, except for initiating trouble for the peasants and then failing in any way to save them from it, advances the viewpoint of those who have asserted that rather than effectively confronting the Japanese, Mao primarily spent his energy playing the Japanese and the Nationalists off against each other to his own narrow advantage. In this view, the essential strategy of the Long March to northern Shaanxi province was to fall behind Japanese lines and use the Japanese position as a protective screen against Chiang Kai-shek's forces. Decades later, on September 27, 1972, when Japanese Prime Minister Tanaka Kakuei came to Beijing to transfer diplomatic recognition from the Taiwan government to the People's Republic, the official communiqué registered his public expression, carefully understated as usual, that "The Japanese side is keenly conscious of the responsibility for the serious damage that Japan caused in the past to the Chinese people." Mao's officially promulgated reply was that "If Japan hadn't invaded China, the Chinese Communist

Party would not have been victorious, moreover we would never be meeting today. This is the dialectic of history."[147]

Who is the Devil?

Built on a series of role reversals and power shifts between captors and captives, *Devils on the Doorstep* is a contemplation on ethical values as well as a study of what social psychologist Philip Zimbardo has labeled "situational power."[148] While still a captive, Ma Dasan finds himself fortuitously thrust into the role of captor. For some reason—because he is a morally just man, or because he has never possessed power over others and is culturally conditioned to passivity, or because he is too much a coward, or because he fears that committing murder while his unborn child is still in the womb will pollute his offspring, or perhaps some algorithm of all these—he does not simply reverse roles with his captors and victimize his captives, contrary to what psychologists suggest one might normally expect.[149] In Zimbardo's renowned Stanford Prison Experiment of 1971, a group of psychologically "normal" college students who were arbitrarily assigned to the roles of guards and prisoners adapted within hours to the functions of sadistic victimizers and passive victims. "I practically considered the prisoners 'cattle,'" admitted one captor.[150] The readiness of participants to identify with their assigned teams and conform to their roles astounded the researchers, and the ferocity with which the guards carried out their functions required that the experiment be cut short in less than half the planned study time. One of Zimbardo's student guards said afterward:

> Once you put a uniform on, and are given a role, I mean, a job, saying "Your job is to keep these people in line," then you're certainly not the same person if you're in street clothes and in a different role. You really become that person once you put on the khaki uniform, you put on the glasses, you take the nightstick, and you act the part. That's your costume and you have to act accordingly when you put it on.[151]

The fluidity of the subjects' change in behavior was striking but not for the better, whether guard or prisoner; imprisonment, like warfare, creates a damned-if-you-do, damned-if-you-don't condition.

Zimbardo believes that the population of those capable of avoiding such role-identification is small:

> There were always some individuals who resisted, who did not yield to temptation. What delivered them from evil was not some inherent magical goodness but rather, more likely, an understanding, however intuitive, of mental and social tactics of resistance.[152]

For whatever reasons, Ma Dasan is one of those few, throughout most of the film resisting affiliation as captor or captive. His encounter with Hanaya leads to a surprise bonding between peasants, Chinese and Japanese, class solidarity overriding nationalist enmity. Optimistic but naive, Ma Dasan projects this experience onto his captors; he convinces himself that they are not essentially that different from himself and not that bad after all, that they are really more "banal" than they are irredeemably evil,[153] that they can be dealt with on more or less equal terms and their evil negated. Ma Dasan's experience leads him to behave as if the enemy's worst behavior is situationally determined rather than innate and immutable, consistent with Zimbardo's imprisonment situation in which

> Neither the guards nor the prisoners could be considered "bad apples" prior to the time when they were so powerfully impacted by being embedded in a "bad barrel".... They were not the proverbial "bad apples" — rather, it was the "bad barrel" of the Stanford prison that was implicated in the transformations that had been demonstrated so vividly.[154]

For Ma Dasan, *Devils on the Doorstep*, and Jiang Wen, there exists no essential moral difference between the Japanese and Chinese *as individuals*, but for the varying circumstances and the systems of militarism and captivity that operate upon them. Rather than explaining *why* the Japanese are guards and the Chinese are prisoners in this "experiment," it suggests (above all, through Ma Dasan's own violence) that this is merely historical circumstance and over time is reversible. This is hardly an agreeable historical attitude from the point of view of today's Chinese government (although how else is one to understand territorial expansion in China's own "Golden Ages" of imperialism or its modern conquest of Tibet?) and helps to explain the severity of the official response to the rhetorical position of this film.

Drawing ethical conclusions from psychological data, Philip Zimbardo claims that

> We overemphasize personality in explaining any behavior while concurrently underemphasizing situational influences.... Any deed that any human being has ever committed, however horrible, is possible for any of us — under the right or wrong situational circumstances. That knowledge does not excuse evil; rather, it democratizes it, sharing its blame among ordinary actors rather than declaring it the province only of deviants and despots — of Them but not Us. The primary simple lesson the Stanford Prison Experiment teaches is that *situations matter*. Social situations can have more profound effects on the behavior and mental functioning of individuals, groups, and national leaders than we might believe possible. Some situations can exert such powerful influence over us that we can be led to behave in ways we would not, could not, predict was possible in advance.[155]

Reservations about the historical ethics of this "situational" view are expressed by Daqing Yang:

> Most Chinese accounts of the Nanjing Massacre have ended with a simple political message: the revival of militarism in Japan must be stopped and the Japanese government has to atone for the country's past aggression against China. Although the majority of Japanese do consider the moral implications of an atrocity like the Nanjing Massacre, many do so only in a universal way, to the extent that perpetrators and victims become indistinguishable. Much has been made of the fact that General Matsui Iwane, upon return to Japan, built an altar dedicated to the fallen Japanese and Chinese soldiers in Nanjing. When this mode is applied to historical inquiry, however, it can lead to what Charles Maier calls Bitburg History. Such an approach, as Maier describes it, "Unites oppressors and victims...in a common dialectic" and makes it difficult to pin down any notion of collective responsibility. Many Japanese ex-soldiers who testified to the atrocity in Nanjing put the blame squarely on the war. Former sergeant Ide Junji, who recalled witnessing brutal killings in Nanjing by the Japanese troops, put it as well as anyone else: "Human beings are capable of being god and demon. It is war that induces human beings to

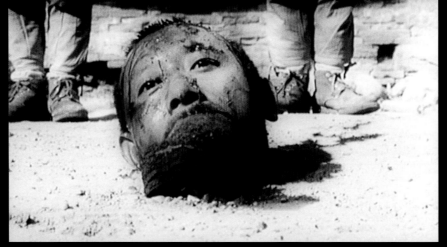

[071]

Dasan beheaded

become demons." There is certainly truth in such a statement, and sentiments like this are genuine and have contributed to the strong pacifism in postwar Japan. War is indeed responsible for many human excesses. However, blaming everything on the war is at best inadequate and at worst can be used as an excuse to avoid confronting the crucial issue of agency, for even in the most brutal of wars not everyone killed or raped civilians. Acknowledgment of the dehumanizing impact of war, although highly important, cannot replace a critical analysis of the individual decisions as well as the particular political institutions.[156]

Ma Dasan chooses to adopt a "situational" or "universal" view of wartime responsibility, and perhaps he is not wrong in this, but he fails to recognize that his own behavior is also situational and that in the worst of circumstances — the Japanese-led massacre and the Chinese-led executions at the end of the film — he is just as capable as the others of unpredictable violence. It is through this sympathetic character that Jiang Wen "democratizes" the devilishness of warfare. Competing, negotiating, almost toying with the enemy and temporarily emerging triumphant, Ma Dasan exaggerates the fluidity of situational roles and misjudges the essential relationship between captor and captive; he underestimates his captors' culture of violence and fails to fully anticipate its danger. It is only when this failed judgment is made apparent and through his own horrible descent into violence that Ma Dasan loses all hope for the attainment of social justice in this world and abandons all desire to go on living in such an unjust, morally confusing, and profoundly frustrating universe.[157]

When Ma Dasan's final "statement" comes forth as the braying of a donkey (see frame 069), this is explained by an onlooker (supposedly a former Qing court executioner) as a "cry to Heaven," upon which Ma Dasan dies: the black-and-white film slowly saturates to a rich color (just the opposite of *In the Heat of the Sun*), to a bloody red seen mostly through the victim's eyes as his head rolls across the execution ground [071]. We have already been told that if his head rolls nine times, if his eyes blink three blinks and he smiles, Ma Dasan will trade this crazy, animalistic life on earth for the peace and harmony of Heaven.[158] And he does. ∎

Figure 33 Xu Beihong, *The Foolish Old Man Who Removed the Mountains*, 1939. Oil on paper. Hanhai Art Auction House, June 2006. Author's photograph.

EPILOGUE: TWO FILMS AND THE "TWO MOUNTAINS"

On June 25, 2006, a record was set for the price a Chinese oil painting sold at auction, a price of 33 million yuan or 4.12 million US dollars. (fig. 33) The painting is an early version of the well-known work by Xu Beihong (1895–1953) *The Foolish Old Man Who Removed the Mountains* (*Yugong yi shan*), the final version of which now hangs in the Xu Beihong Memorial Museum in Beijing. Xu Beihong made this first version in Singapore in 1939, where he had gone to raise funds to aid Chinese refugees early in the war against Japan, and he finished the later painting a year afterwards in Darjeeling, on a trip where he met Rabindranath Tagore and Gandhi. It is said that Xu Beihong's early version ended up in a dry well at a school in Singapore, hidden there just before his return to China on the eve of the Japanese attack on Pearl Harbor, that it was recovered ten years later, and only with the auction at Beijing's Hanhai Art Auction House in 2006 did it finally return to mainland Chinese ownership, in a private collection.

Neither version of this painting will seem at all attractive to a Western audience. Michael Sullivan's survey volume on twentieth-century Chinese painting describes the final version, done in ink and color on paper, as "uncomfortable and tasteless."[159] The record auction price may therefore seem puzzling, but the value of the work derives not from any hidden stylistic virtues and rather from its subject matter and its subsequent connection to Party Chairman Mao Zedong, under whom Xu Beihong would be appointed the president of the Central Academy of Fine Arts in Beijing and first chairman of the Chinese Artists Association.

The Chinese Communist Party bases its historical claim to authority on two propositions: first, that it rid "semi-colonial" China of foreign imperialism with its expulsion of invading Japanese and native Guomindang Nationalists, the latter regarded as an American "puppet" regime which refused to fight the Japanese and attacked only their Communist fellow-countrymen; and second, that it overthrew China's old "semi-feudal, semi-bourgeois" political economy with a revolutionary egalitarian order. This dual elimination was the topic of Mao Zedong's famous speech made in 1945 that appropriated the famous legend of "The Foolish Old Man." Mao's speech went as follows:

> There is an ancient Chinese fable called "The Foolish Old Man Who Removed the Mountains." It tells of an old man who lived in northern China long, long ago and was known as the Foolish Old Man of North Mountain. His house faced south and beyond his doorway stood the two great peaks, Taihang and Wangwu, obstructing the way. He called his sons, and hoe in hand they began to dig up these mountains with great determination. Another gray-beard, known as the Wise Old Man, saw them and said derisively, "How silly of you to do this! It is quite impossible for you few to dig up those two huge mountains." The Foolish Old Man replied, "When I die, my sons will carry on; when they die, there will be my grandsons, and then their sons and grand-sons, and so on to infinity. High as they are, the mountains cannot grow any higher and with every bit we dig, they will be that much lower. Why can't we clear them away?" Having refuted the Wise Old Man's wrong view, he went on digging every day, unshaken in his conviction. God was moved by this, and he sent down two angels, who carried the mountains away on their backs. Today, two big mountains lie like a dead weight on the Chinese people. One is imperialism, the other is feudalism. The Chinese Communist Party has long made up its mind to dig them up. We must persevere and work unceasingly, and we, too, will touch God's heart. Our God is none other than the masses of the Chinese people. If they stand up and dig together with us, why can't these two mountains be cleared away?[160]

Strikingly, these two poles of legitimacy—Mao's two "mountains," the founding myth of Communist China, enshrining early on Mao's notion of per-manent revolution—constitute the two central targets of Jiang Wen's two films: the myth of equality is undermined in *In the Heat of the Sun*, and the anti-Japanese resistance narrative is deconstructed in *Devils on the Door-step*. As anyone remotely interested in China will be aware, since the late 1970s the pursuit of economic equity, of a classless society, has been, at the very least, deferred; the command-economy and central control of everything other than politics and the military has given way to capital formation based on a market economy, so that the Party's wartime claims must continually be recalled to mind and unsatisfied antagonisms with Japan must repeatedly be aroused.[161] Jiang Wen's critique is more radical than this. Through its depiction of the Party elite, *In the Heat of the Sun* dares to suggest that except as ideology, myth or false memory, equality never existed.[162] As for the Party's continuing claims to wartime heroics, *Devils* suggests that such boasts are as illusory as ghosts.[163]

History is a record of continuities; many of its events that seem discontinuous or unrelated really are not so. After completing this text, I met with Jiang Wen to confirm the views expressed here. At the very end of our time together, I asked what happened at the conclusion of *Devils on the Doorstep* to Yu'er, who disappears entirely from the last portion of the film's narrative, following the massacre of Chinese villagers at Rack-Armor Terrace. Jiang explained that since she was pregnant at the time, she would have given birth and followed the traditional practice of lying-in, remaining bed-bound for some time afterwards, so she would not have been present for Ma Dasan's tragic demise. And then, Jiang Wen asked, do you know who her baby was? His answer: it might have been, in *In the Heat of the Sun*, Ma Xiaojun's father. ∎

Notes

1. Jiang Wen (b. 1963, Beijing) graduated in 1984 from the Central Academy of Drama in Beijing, where he now continues to hold the rank of research professor. On his role in *Hibiscus Town* (director Xie Jin, 1986), see Jerome Silbergeld, *China Into Film: Frames of Reference in Contemporary Chinese Cinema* (London: Reaktion Books, 1999), chapter 5 ("The Force of Labels: Melodrama in the Modern Era"); on *Red Sorghum* (director Zhang Yimou, 1987), see ibid., chapter 2 ("Ruins of a Sorghum Field, Eclipse of a Nation: *Red Sorghum* on Page and Screen").

2. Gu Changwei (b. 1957, Xi'an), a "fifth generation" graduate of the Beijing Film Academy's cinematography department in 1982. If any director ever deserved the inflated title "auteur" it would be Jiang Wen, but in pairing himself with Gu Changwei, Jiang Wen put his early directorial efforts in the hands of a mature cinematic master. Largely unknown in the West, Gu was the cinematographer of such notable earlier films as *King of the Children* (director Chen Kaige, 1987) and *Red Sorghum* (director Zhang Yimou, 1987), two films which jointly earned him a Chinese Golden Rooster Award; *Judou* (director Zhang Yimou, 1990); *Life on a String* (director Chen Kaige, 1991); and *Farewell My Concubine* (director Chen Kaige, 1993), for which Gu Changwei won an Academy Award nomination. In 2004, Gu Changwei directed and coproduced his own first film, *Peacock* (*Kongque*), for which he won the Jury Grand Prix Silver Bear at the Berlin International Film Festival.

3. Xia Yu (b. 1978), a striking younger look-alike for Jiang Wen, won the best actor award for *In the Heat of the Sun* at the Venice Film Festival, the youngest actor to win that award, and has gone on to a successful acting career in films including *Shadow Magic* (director Ann Hu, 2000).

4. Gu Changning worked on earlier films including *Red Sorghum* (sound designer, for which he won the Golden Rooster award; director Zhang Yimou, 1987); *King of the Children* (sound designer; director Chen Kaige, 1987); *Red Firecracker, Green Firecracker* (musical director and sound designer; director He Ping, 1994); and *The Sun Has Ears* (sound designer; director Yim Ho, 1996).

5. Having moved to France, Jiang Wen refused to direct another film until he could do so in China. He returned to China and began directing a new film in October 2005, *The Sun Also Rises* (*Taiyang zhaochang shengqi*), which was completed in the autumn of 2007 and distributed as this book was going to press. Jiang Wen was not proscribed from further acting roles, and in the interim starred in several films, including *The Missing Gun* (director Lu Chuan, 2002), *Green Tea* (director Zhang Yuan, 2003), *Warriors of Heaven and Earth* (director He Ping, 2003), and *Jasmine Women* (director Hou Yong, 2004).

6. Cf. Zhang Zhen, ed., *The Urban Generation: Chinese Cinema and Society at the Turn of the Twenty-first Century* (Durham: Duke University Press, 2007); also, Paul G. Pickowicz and Yingjin Zhang, eds., *From Underground to Independent: Alternative Film Culture in Contemporary China* (Lanham, MD: Rowman and Littlefield, 2006).

7. Wu Hung and Katherine R. Tsiang, eds., *Body and Face in Chinese Visual Culture* (Cambridge, MA: Harvard University Asia Center; Harvard University Press, 2005).

8. John Hay, "Values and History in Chinese Painting: Hsieh Ho Revisited and the Hierarchic Evolution of Structure," *Res 6* (Fall 1983), 73–111, and *Res* 7/8 (Spring/ Autumn 1984), 102–36. John Hay, *Kernels of Energy, Bones of Earth: The Rock in Chinese Art* (New York: China Institute in America, 1985).

9. Cary Liu, "Chinese Architectural Aesthetics: Patterns of Living and Being between Past and Present," in Ronald Knapp and Kai–yin Lo, eds., *House Home Family: Living and Being Chinese* (Honolulu: University of Hawai'i Press; New York: China Institute in America, 2005), 142.

10. The Chinese filmgoing viewer will be reminded by this public encounter of director Zhang Yimou's *Story of Qiu Ju* (1992), made shortly after the authoritarian outrage at Tianamen, based on Chen Yuanbin's novella, *Wan jia susong* (*The Wan Family's Lawsuit*). See Silbergeld, *China Into Film*, 120–31.

11. Jerome Silbergeld, *Hitchcock with a Chinese Face: Cinematic Doubles, Oedipal Triangles, and China's Moral Voice* (Seattle and London: University of Washington Press, 2004), 8.

12. For studies of anthropomorphism in Chinese painting, see Chu-tsing Li, "The Freer *Sheep and Goat* and Chao Meng-fu's Horse Paintings," *Artibus Asiae* 30.4 (1968), 229–326, 337–46; Jerome Silbergeld, "In Praise of Government: Chao Yung's Painting, *Noble Steeds*, and Late Yüan Politics," *Artibus Asiae* 46.3 (1985), 159–202.

13. This simple notion is engaged theoretically by Angela Zito and Tani E. Barlow throughout the introduction to their volume *Body, Subject, and Power in China* (Chicago: University of Chicago Press, 1994), where they write that "It is important to distinguish carefully what we mean when we substitute 'subjectivity' and 'subject positionality' for older words like mind, consciousness, or subject. These older usages carry the sense that the person is a fixed essence because personality is to human organism as culture is to nature. Subjectivity and subject positionality are part of a vocabulary of twentieth-century critical theory, the core of which is Marx's nineteenth-century insight that human beings are engaged in and produced through social life" (8).

14. Pierre Corneille, *The Theatre of Illusion*, trans. Richard Wilbur (Orlando, FL: Harcourt, 2007), 118.

15. Jean Baptiste Poquelin de Molière, *The Misanthrope and Tartuffe*, trans. Richard Wilbur (Orlando, FL: Harcourt, 1965), 173.

16. Wang Shuo (b. 1958), also screenwriter for *The Trouble-Shooters* (or, *The Operators*; director Mi Jiashan, 1988) and *Samsara/Transmigration* (director Huang Jianxin, 1988); cf. Silbergeld, *China Into Film*, 86–89, 94–95. See Geremie Barmé, "Wang Shuo and Hooligan ('Liumang') Culture," *Australian Journal of Chinese Affairs* 28 (July 1992), 23–64; Geremie Barmé, *In the Red: On Contemporary Chinese Culture* (New York: Columbia University Press, 1999), especially chapter 4, "The Apotheosis of the *Liumang*." Wang Shuo was born to a disciplinarian military father, whom he discovered had served the Japanese as a police officer during the war, which set the stage early for his distrust of authority and its facades ("Given his father's dubious past, it was only natural that Wang Shuo's rebellion began at home," wrote critic Zuo Shula). Critics have "declared that Wang's favorite characters were nothing less than 'potential criminals'" and that in his writings, "Life can no longer be understood in terms of black and white or good and bad. With Wang Shuo we enter a state of confusion." Barmé, *In the Red*, 70–71.

17. Wang Shuo, *Dongwu xiongmeng* (*Wild Beasts*), originally published in the literary journal *Shouhuo* 1992.6 (1991), 130–69;

subsequently published in book form, Hong Kong: Chuangjian chuban youxian gongsi, 1994; also, Beijing: Taihai chubanshe, 2001. Coincidentally, Wang Shuo moved across the street in Beijing from Jiang Wen in 1991 and discussed the book extensively with him, but emphasizes his distance from the film. "I refused to produce a screenplay.... I was suffering writer's block. I especially detest writing screenplays for ambitious directors...and there was no way I was going to help Jiang Wen transform this novel into a film narrative. This would have to come from his own creativity. To this day I still believe the director ought to write his own screenplay." Wang Shuo, "*Yangguang canlan de rizi zhuiyi*" ("Recollections of *In the Heat of the Sun*"), *Ashu dianying gushi* 528, <ashu528.diy.myrice.com/myhome/topic/topic-006.htm>; for this complete text, see Wang Shuo, "*Yangguang canlan de rizi zhuiyi,*" in Jiang Wen et al., *Yibu dianying de dansheng* (*The Birth of a Film*) (Beijing: Huayi chubanshe, 1997), 430–513. See note 74 below for an enumeration of significant differences between text and film, which make the latter seem more the creation of Jiang Wen than of Wang Shuo. In the film, Wang Shuo appears as a youth-gang leader, Xiao Huaidan, who prefers revelry to fighting and who falls prey to ambitious gang members seeking their way to the top. For Jiang's confirmation of the film's autobiographical intent, see the online interview by Wei Xidi, "*Jiang Wen zhangdale*" ("Jiang Wen Matures"), <www.filmsea.com.cn/celebrity_review/200112071223.htm>, dated December 7, 2000. (All Websites cited herein were accessed between January 1 and February 1, 2007.) For Jiang Wen's own notes on the film, see his *Yibu dianying de dansheng* (The Birth of a Film).

18. See Silbergeld, *China Into Film*, for discussions of each of these films.

19. Referred to as *da yuan wenhua*, "big courtyard culture," for their large, well-provisioned residences, hidden behind high walls in elite residential districts.

20. Jiang Wen confirms that the film's narrative voice is his own; personal communication.

21. Yomi Braester has dealt effectively in publication with aspects of memory and subversion in this film, in *Witness Against History: Literature, Film, and Public Discourse in Twentieth-Century China* (Stanford: Stanford University Press, 2003), 192–205.

22. Yingjin Zhang, *Screening China: Critical Interventions, Cinematic Reconfigurations, and the Transnational Imaginary in Contemporary Chinese Cinema* (Ann Arbor: Center for Chinese Studies, University of Michigan, 2002), 12.

23. Interview by Brian Bennett, "Back in Action," *TIME Asia Magazine* 159.24, June 17, 2002, <www.time.com/time/asia/magazine/printout/0,13675,501020624-263045,00.html>.

24. Corneille, *The Theater of Illusion*; see also Pierre Corneille, freely adapted by Tony Kushner, *The Illusion* (New York: Theater Communications Group, 1994). John Trethewey writes that this play is primarily "an advertisement for theatre, and as a demonstration of its power to captivate." It requires of the audience, he writes, a "suspension of disbelief." "[Its] form was, it has been suggested, prevalent—together with other forms of what is today termed 'reflexive theatre' or 'metatheatre'—in the baroque period and has manifested itself at other times when the art has felt the need to examine itself and the validity of its current assumptions and conventions." John Trethewey, *Corneille: L'Illusion Comique and Le Menteur* (London: Grant and Cutler, 1991), 30, 26, 16. The critique of *In the Heat of the Sun*, by contrast, seems to deny any meaningful differentiation between the staging of theater and the theatrics of society.

25. Pierre Corneille, ed. Robert Garapon, *L'Illusion comique, comédie, publiée d'après la première édition (1639) avec les variantes* (Paris: Librairie Nizet, 1985), 3.

26. Internet Movie Database user review submitted on October 29, 2003, <www.us .imdb.com/title/tt0111786>.

27. For examples of each period, see Jerome Silbergeld, "In Praise of Government"; Silbergeld, "Kung Hsien's Self-Portrait in Willows, With Notes on the Willow in Chinese Painting and Literature," *Artibus Asiae* 42.1 (1980), 5–38.

28. Silbergeld, *China Into Film*, 260–82.

29. Mark Twain, *The Adventures of Tom Sawyer* (New York: Grosset and Dunlap, 1946), 188–89.

30. The popular star Ning Jing is said to have gained thirty pounds for this role.

31. Mao's best description of the concept, perhaps, came in 1942, more than a decade before he actually adopted the term: "Although man's social life is the only source of literature and art and is incomparably livelier and richer in content, the people are not satisfied with life alone and demand literature and art as well. Why? Because, while both are beautiful, life as reflected in works of literature and art can and ought to be on a higher plane, more intense, more concentrated, more typical, nearer the ideal, and therefore more universal than actual everyday life. Revolutionary literature and art should create a variety of characters out of real life and help the masses to prod history forward." Mao Zedong, *Talks at the Yenan Forum on Literature and Art* (Beijing: Foreign Languages Press, 1967), 19.

32. Qu Yuan, "The Nine Songs," in Arthur Waley, translator, *The Nine Songs: A Study in Shamanism in Ancient China* (London:

G. Allen and Unwin, 1955); and, in David Hawkes, translator, *Ch'u Tz'u, The Songs of the South: An Ancient Chinese Anthology* (Oxford: Oxford University Press, 1959), 35–44.

33. Leo Steinberg, *The Sexuality of Christ in Renaissance Art and in Modern Oblivion* (2nd edition, revised; Chicago: University of Chicago Press, 1993).

34. E.g., Anita Chan, *Children of Mao: Personality Development and Political Activism in the Red Guard Generation* (Seattle and London: University of Washington Press, 1985).

35. Chen Xiaomei, "Growing Up With Posters in the Maoist Era," in Harriet Evans and Stephanie Donald, eds., *Picturing Power in the People's Republic of China: Posters of the Cultural Revolution* (Lanham, MD: Rowman and Littlefield, 1999), 111–12.

36. In Bennett, "Back in Action."

37. Yomi Braester (alone, as far as I know) recognizes this equation, writing briefly that "the infatuated Xiaojun shapes Mi Lan as a sensuous version of Mao, the object of adoration at the time" (205). For the opposite — and widely prevalent — view, see Yingjin Zhang, *Screening China*, 12; or Wendy Larson, "'Anything Can Happen': Remembering the Future in 'In the Heat of the Sun,'" unpublished paper delivered at the conference on "Rethinking Cultural Revolution Culture," Heidelberg, February 2001, which sees Ma Xiaojun's mentality, and thus the film's own viewpoint, as "shifted out of the revolutionary sphere and into the personal, sexual arena...innocent and charming...an idealistic mental state that belies and challenges any contrast from the material world" (2). Tonglin Lu's "Lacanian/Žižekian reading" of the erotics of Cultural Revolution violence views Jiang Wen's work as "[putting] the image of the Great Leader and the phallus on the same

level" but as "ideologically...fragmentary."
"Fantasy and Ideology in a Chinese Film: A
Žižekian Reading of the Cultural Revolution,"
Positions 12.2 [Fall 2004], 554, 551. See
also Shuqin Cui's treatment of the film's
adolescent psychology in relation to Jiang
Wen's generation of filmmakers, "Working
from the Margins: Urban Cinema and
Independent Directors in Contemporary
China," in Sheldon Lu and Emelie Yueh-yu
Yeh, eds., *Chinese Language Film: Historiog-
raphy, Poetics, Politics* (Honolulu: University
of Hawai'i Press, 2005), 112–16.

38. Quoted in Geremie Barmé, ed., *Shades of
Mao: The Posthumous Cult of the Great Leader*
(Armonk, NY: M.E. Sharpe, 1996), 171.

39. Li Zhisui, *The Private Life of Chairman
Mao: The Memoirs of Mao's Personal Physician*,
trans. Dai Hongzhao and Anne F. Thurston
(1994; Armonk, NY: M.E. Sharpe, 1996), 363.
According to Li, Mao's affairs were secretly
tape-recorded by senior Politburo colleagues
during his partial political eclipse in the
early 1960s (292–93, 365–69).

40. Li Shan (b. 1941, Heilongjiang province),
a graduate of the Shanghai Drama Academy's
Department of Oil Painting, 1968, taught
there until his retirement after 2000.

41. Mao insisted on wearing a cap for this
photo, so Snow put his own cap on Mao.
For a photograph of Snow in that battered
military cap, see Lois Wheeler Snow, comp.,
*Edgar Snow's China: A Personal Account of
the Chinese Revolution Compiled from the
Writings of Edgar Snow* (New York: Random
House, 1981), 132.

42. Cf. the "Guanyin as Seductress" section
of Chün-fang Yü, "Guanyin: The Chinese
Transformation of Avalokiteshvara," in
Marsha Weidner, ed., *Latter Days of the
Law: Images of Chinese Buddhism, 850–1850*
(Lawrence: Spencer Museum of Art,
University of Kansas; Honolulu: University
of Hawaii Press, 1994), 166–69.

43. Compare yet another Snow photograph
of a tired-looking Mao at Baoan, in Edgar
Snow, *Red Star Over China* (London: Victor
Gollancz, 1937), following 224.

44. On Mao's womanizing in his youthful
Yan'an years, see Jung Chang and Jon
Halliday, *Mao: The Unknown Story* (New York:
Alfred A. Knopf, 2005), chapter 18.

45. Robert Graves, *I, Claudius: From the
Autobiography of Tiberius Claudius, Born
B.C. X, Murdered and Deified A.D. LIV* (New
York: Random House, 1961), 423.

46. Karen Smith, in an extensive discussion
of Li Shan's work, emphasizes the homo-
erotic aspects of the *Rouge* series. Karen
Smith, *Nine Lives: The Birth of Avant-Garde
Art in China* (Zürich: Scalo, 2005), 221–59. Li
Shan had this to say about the subject, "I am
motivated by the delicate balance that exists
between perversity and power, power and
perversity. This is the rationale behind the
Rouge series.... Power must have an object
over which to wield its strength. Within the
grey areas of morality, alternative sexuality is doomed to be the target of those in
power. They will not destroy it, since power
without a target has no way to demonstrate
its power. Thus, the object becomes a play-
thing in the hand of power" (in Smith, 250).

47. Wang Shuo, *Dongwu xiongmeng*, 37;
Braester, *Witness Against History*, 205.

48. James Agee, *Agee on Film: Reviews
and Comments by James Agee* (New York:
Beacon, 1985), 329.

49. Pietro Mascagni, "Prelude" to *Cavalliera
Rusticana*, 1889.

50. Cf. Braester, *Witness Against History*, 198.

51. The capacity simply to recognize a visual
image and distinguish it from a similar one
not previously seen is remarkable, with
a median recognition rate of 98.5 percent
accuracy achieved by subjects comparing
over six hundred pairs; cf. Roger Shepard's
work on visual recognition, surprising

at the time, "Recognition Memory for Words, Sentences, and Pictures," *Journal of Verbal Learning and Verbal Behavior* 6 (1967), 156–63; also Richard D. Freund, "Verbal and Non-verbal Processes in Picture Recognition," Ph.D. dissertation, Stanford University, 1972. However, on more complex aspects of visual memory, see Ira E. Hyman and Elizabeth F. Loftus, "Errors in Autobiographical Memory," *Clinical Psychology Review* 18.8 (December 1998), 933–47, which concludes, "Memory is always constructive. People create the past based on the information that remains in memory, their general knowledge, and the social demands of the retrieval situation" (933). For some of Loftus's work and reviews of the work in this field, see her *Eyewitness Testimony* (Cambridge MA: Harvard University Press, 1979); Loftus and Edith Green, "Warning: Even Memory for Faces May Be Contagious," *Law and Human Behavior* 4.4 (1980), 323–34; Loftus, "Memory and Its Distortions," in Alan G. Kraut, ed. *The G. Stanley Hall Lecture Series, 2* (Washington, DC: American Psychological Association, 1982), 123–54; Loftus, "Manufacturing Memory," *American Journal of Forensic Psychology* 16.2 (1998), 63–75.

52. Kathryn Braun et al., "Make My Memory: How Advertising Can Change Our Memories of the Past," *Psychology and Marketing* 19.1 (January 2002), 1–23.

53. My article on this topic, "The Photograph in the Movie: On the Boundaries of Cinematography, Photography, and Videography," is forthcoming in *Bridges to Heaven: Essays on East Asian Art in Honor of Professor Wen C. Fong*, ed. Jerome Silbergeld, Dora C.Y. Ching, Alfreda Murck, and Judith G. Smith (Princeton: Princeton University Press).

54. Wang Shuo was 33 when he wrote the story; Jiang Wen was 37 when the film was completed.

55. The Czechoslovakian flag (and now the flag of the Czech Republic) is white above, red below, and overlapped on the left side by a blue triangle. The flag beside Mi Lan's photo is blue above, white below, with a red triangle.

56. The film begins in 1959, with Ma Xiaojun at about age of seven or eight; when this episode takes place, late in the Cultural Revolution, no more than seven years later and likely even less, Xiaojun would have been about fourteen. Actor Xia Yu was about sixteen when the film was made and seventeen when he received the Venice Film Festival best actor's award for it.

57. Tonglin Lu, "Fantasy and Ideology in a Chinese Film," 552, also notes this flag but, strangely, identifies it as Albanian and invents an "Albanian" diplomat to go with it, although the Albanian flag then and always has featured a double-headed black eagle on a red ground. Elsewhere, she inadvertently transforms a Lincoln limousine into a Cadillac (550) and turns a urinating Teacher Hu into a masturbator (552).

58. Personal communication.

59. See Britta Erickson, *The Art of Xu Bing: Words Without Meaning, Meaning Without Words* (Washington, DC: Arthur M. Sackler Gallery, Smithsonian Institution; Seattle and London: University of Washington Press, 2001.

60. *Red Detachment of Women* (director Xie Jin, 1961); *Lenin in 1918* (directors E. Aron, Mikhail Romm, L. Simkov, 1939).

61. I have not managed to identify this film, and Jiang Wen (personal communication) has told me that he does not remember its name: "It's just some popular late-70s film that a friend once imported for restricted study."

62. Yiku, appropriately, means "Remembering Bitterness." His brother is named Liu Sitian, "Thinking of Sweetness."

63. Braester, *Witness Against History*, 196.

64. Wu Hung, *The Double Screen: Medium and Representation in Chinese Painting* (Chicago: University of Chicago Press, 1996), 78, 84, 102, and 129.

65. William Shakespeare, *The Merchant of Venice*, in *Shakespeare, The Complete Works*, ed. G.B. Harrison (New York: Harcourt, Brace, and World, 1968), 604. Oscar Wilde, "The Ballad of Reading Gaol" (1898), in *The Complete Works of Oscar Wilde* (New York: Harper and Row, 1989), 844. Alfred Hitchcock kept the literary lineage alive into a later generation; while discussing the characters' motivation in *North by Northwest* — hero Roger Thornhill (Cary Grant) seems to want heroine Eve Kendall (Eva Marie Saint) dead — he mused, "What's that old Oscar Wilde thing? 'Each man kills the thing he loves....' That I think is a very natural phenomenon, really." In Sidney Gottlieb, ed., *Alfred Hitchcock Interviews* (Jackson: University Press of Mississippi, 2003), 51.

66. Yingjin Zhang tells me that this scene was cut from the theater version he watched at Beijing University in 1995.

67. Mascagni's romantic "Prelude" to *Cavalliera* is also used widely throughout this film, beginning the moment Xiaojun first sees the photo of Mi Lan. This music also figures prominently in another ballad of a winner-turned-loser, Martin Scorsese's *Raging Bull* (1980), a film Jiang Wen knows well.

68. See Silbergeld, *Hitchcock with a Chinese Face*, chapter 3 ("The Chinese Heart in Conflict with Itself: *Good Men, Good Women*").

69. In *Woman from the Lake of Scented Souls* (director Xie Fei, 1993), the failure of the film's lead character, Xiang Ersao (Siqin Gaowa), to shield her retarded and epileptic son from the public, her insistence on treating him as normal, brings about both her own family's downfall and that of his bride's family. See Silbergeld, *China Into Film*, 170–86. Gu Changwei's film *Peacock* deals in part with such a child. For some observations on the extension of this stigma into the Chinese-American community, in an account of the author Iris Chang, whose bipolar disorder led to suicide, see Paula Kamen, *Finding Iris Chang: Friendship, Ambition, and the Loss of an Extraordinary Mind* (Philadelphia: Da Capo Press, 2007), especially 220–26.

70. This childhood character is reminiscent of the idiot Benjy from Faulkner's *The Sound and the Fury*, now so popular in China.

71. I am indebted to Carma Hinton for the expansion of my Chinese vocabulary.

72. Although the occupants of the limousine are not clearly distinguished from each other, the film credits make clear which ones of them are present here.

73. Silbergeld, *Hitchcock with a Chinese Face*, chapters 1 ("Hitchcock with a Chinese Face: *Suzhou River*") and 3.

74. The changes wrought by Jiang Wen on Wang Shuo's original tale are numerous and telling: the classroom scene early in the film, Ma Xiaojun's wearing of his father's military medals, his fateful play with his father's condom, Xiaojun and his friend parodying the events in the Soviet film *Lenin in 1918* and Xiaojun climbing the smokestack, Party cadres watching the imported nude film scene, the gathering of gangs for a fight beneath the bridge, the character Gulunmu, and the final scene with the limousine are all Jiang Wen's creations, not found in the book. I am grateful to Lanjun Xu at Princeton University for discussing these adaptations with me.

75. Among my own writings, see "In Praise of Government"; "Kung Hsien's Self-Portrait in Willows"; and "Back to the Red Cliff: Reflections on the Narrative Mode in Early

NOTES

Literati Landscape Painting," *Ars Orientalis* 25 (1995), 19–38. Cf. also Hans H. Frankel, *The Flowering Plum and the Palace Lady: Interpretations of Chinese Poetry* (New Haven, CT: Yale University Press, 1976); James J.Y. Liu, *The Art of Chinese Poetry* (Chicago: University of Chicago Press, 1962).

76. Jiang Wen: "The only thing we took from [You Fengwei's] original story was the delivery of the two prisoners. What we wrote was, in effect, an original screenplay." Jiang Wen, interview with Tony Rayns, April 17, 2000, in DVD liner notes, Home Vision Entertainment, distributor.

77. In Philip Zimbardo, *The Lucifer Effect: Understanding How Good People Turn Evil* (New York: Random House, 2007), 213.

78. George Orwell, *Animal Farm* (New York: Harcourt Brace Jovanovich, 1946), 128.

79. Hong Hao (b. 1965, Beijing), educated at the Central Academy of Fine Arts, Beijing.

80. For a pivotal exhibition shown in New York's International Center of Photography and Asia Society Galleries; Chicago's Smart Museum of Art and Museum of Contemporary Art; the Seattle Art Museum; the Victoria and Albert Museum in London; Berlin's Haus der Kulturen der Welt; and the Santa Barbara Museum of Art, see Wu Hung and Christopher Phillips, *Between Past and Future: New Photography and Video From China* (Chicago: Smart Museum of Art, University of Chicago; New York: International Center of Photography; Göttigen: Steidl Publishers, 2004). For an exhibition review, see Holland Cotter, "Like a Bird in Flight: Capturing Today's Chinese Culture in Transition," *New York Times*, June 11, 2004, E41. Hong Hao's photograph was included in this exhibition, as well as in the contemporaneous exhibition *A Strange Heaven,* shown in Prague and Helsinki; see Petr Nedoma and Chang Tsong-zung, *A Strange Heaven: Contemporary*

Chinese Photography (Hong Kong: Asia Art Archive, 2003), 60–63. For the photographic capturing of "ephemeral" but carefully staged performance pieces in an earlier exhibition, see Gao Minglu, ed., *Inside Out: New Chinese Art* (San Francisco: San Francisco Museum of Modern Art; New York: Asia Society Galleries; Berkeley and Los Angeles: University of California Press, 1998).

81. Edward Weston, in Susan Sontag, *On Photography* (New York: Farrar, Straus, and Giroux, 1977), 100.

82. This photograph, by Hei Ming (1985), and the several photographs which follow here are part of China's only comprehensive collection of documentary photography, at the Guangdong Museum of Art, included in the first major exhibition (2003–4) and the first publication of such material, six hundred photographs in all, by two hundred-and-fifty photographers: Wang Huangsheng and Hu Wugong, eds., *Zhongguo renben, jishi zai dangdai: Humanism in China, A Contemporary Record of Photography* (Guangzhou: Lingnan meishu chubanshe, 2003). For this project, over a year's time, a team of curators selected among 100,000 photographs by 1,000 photographers, and the selected works then entered the Guangdong collection.

83. October 21, 1925: "I have been photographing our toilet, that glossy enameled receptacle of extraordinary beauty.... I was thrilled—here was every sensuous curve of the 'human form divine' but minus imperfections. Never did the Greeks reach a more significant consummation to their culture, and it somehow reminded me, in the glory of its chaste convolutions and its swelling, sweeping forward movement of finely progressing contours, of the Victory of Samothrace." Edward Weston, *The Daybooks of Edward Weston, I: Mexico*, ed.

148

Nancy Newhall (New York: Aperture Books, 1973), 132.

84. Sontag, *On Photography*, 170–72.

85. See Hu Zhichuan et al., eds., *Zhongguo sheying shi: 1840–1937* (*A History of Chinese Photography: 1840–1937*) (Beijing: Zhongguo sheying chubanshe, 1987); Richard K. Kent, "Fine Art Amateur Photography in Republican-Period Shanghai," in Silbergeld et al., eds., *Bridges to Heaven*, forthcoming.

86. Sontag, *On Photography*, 171, 170.

87. Ibid., 86.

88. Wang Huangsheng, director of the Guangdong Museum of Art, in his preface to the catalogue of this exhibition, begins: "Technological advancements not only lead to the progress of a civilization, but they also help promote new ways of living and looking at life. Among these technological advancements, photography, and its ability to directly record the changes of society in a visual and 'authentic' way, has contributed to humankind's ability to examine the development of civilizations.... For example, when facing the camera, people have been instructed to make certain poses and expressions which have been commonly accepted in a given period of time. The special feelings produced at these moments have been generally regarded as 'authentic' by the viewer. Similarly, photographers have also been accustomed to recording the commonly accepted 'authenticity' when holding a camera." Wang then asserts that "there is a limit to [such] 'authenticity'" and that following China's "opening up," "there erupted a move toward humanization that was previously impeded" and "during this time, Chinese people have changed from existing as a political collective to existing as individual and social people.... This exhibition," he concludes," will attempt to document this evolution." *Zhongguo renben, jishi zai dangdai*, 6–7.

89. Steinberg, *The Sexuality of Christ*. One wonders how Wang Fuchun's photograph would be viewed by Steinberg, who illustrates numerous paintings of Saint Anne with the conspicuously sexualized Christ child (e.g., Steinberg's fig. 9), and who also dealt with the question of infantile erection in some paintings (76–80, 180–84). Steinberg afterwards explained the reluctance in modern times to deal with, let alone even to recognize the ubiquity and the essence, of these works: "For 30 years or more I had seen pictures in which the nudity of the Christ child seemed strangely accented by a genital focus, and I would observe it again in representations of the dead Christ. And what do you do with this kind of observation? Well, you suppress it. If nobody else draws attention to it, why should you? It just isn't good manners.... If you have any breeding at all, you pretend not to notice." In Margaret Moorman, "Leo Steinberg and the Sexuality of Christ," *Art News* 85.3 (March 1985), 78.

90. Shot in 35mm footage by the head of the Hearst Metrotone News's Shanghai Bureau Chief, H.S. Wong, and distributed in newsreels and published as a single frame in Hearst-syndicated newspapers, the "photograph" was published in the *Life Magazine* issue of October 4, 1937, by which time the magazine text estimated that the image had already been viewed by 136 million people around the globe, to enormous political effect. John Faber, *Great News Photos and the Stories Behind Them* (New York: Dover Books, 1978), 74–75.

91. As far as visual "documentation" goes, the Japanese immediately declared H.S. Wong's photo a fake and reportedly put a price on Wong's life. A film frame of the baby with a man said to be Wong is available today as a still photograph (fig. 25) but it is not clear, is he about to pick the baby up or setting him down to be photographed? Subsequent generations of doubters and deniers have held to the belief that the photographer Wong staged the image and that the bombing of civilians waiting to be evacuated from embattled Shanghai was carried out by Nationalist rather than Japanese airplanes, or alternatively that the site was actually a Nationalist staging area, or (strangely enough) both. On the political manipulation of "documentary" film, see David King, *The Commissar Vanishes: The Falsification of Photographs and Art in Stalin's Russia* (New York: Metropolitan Books/Henry Holt and Company, 1997). For documentation of photography retouched for publication in the *Heilongjiang Daily* during the Cultural Revolution, see Li Zhensheng, *Red-Color News Soldier* (London and New York: Phaidon, 2003), 133.

92. Jiang Wen says he educated the Japanese cast members to their task by showing them documentary film about the war. Interview with Tony Rayns. Perhaps the closest comparison to this documentary "look" in modern Chinese cinematography comes from the Anti-Japan War sequences in Hou Hsiao-hsien's *Good Men, Good Women*, although the pacing there is as slow as *Devils* is fast; see Silbergeld, *Hitchcock with a Chinese Face*, chapter 3.

93. Henri Cartier-Bresson, *Henri Cartier-Bresson* (New York: Aperture, 1987), introduction, unpaginated. Originally published in Bresson's *Images à la Sauvette* (*The Decisive Moment*), 1952.

94. The formal style here might be described simply as "real*ism*," or a commitment to *seeming* realistic. In content, there is no attempt to imply the historicity of the narrative. Nor does the style incorporate those features common in documentary film, such as interviews of the characters, the insertion of real people or archival material, or voice-over narration. It corresponds neither to those films labeled as "docudrama" (fictional form plus documentary content, as in *The Battle of Algiers, Raging Bull,* and *Schindler's List*) or "mockumentary" (documentary form plus fictional content, frequently intended to parody the documentary form, in films such as *Dr. Strangelove, Nashville, Zelig, Blue in the Face, A Mighty Wind,* or *The Blair Witch Project*), nor as "faction" (which tends to be limited to television production). Cf. Jane Roscoe and Craig Hight, *Faking It: Mock-documentary and the Subversion of Factuality* (Manchester and New York: Manchester University Press, 2001); Gary D. Rhodes and John Parris Springer, eds., *Docufictions: Essays on the Intersection of Documentary and Fictional Filmmaking* (Jefferson, NC, and London: McFarland and Company, 2006).

95. In the development of Chinese conceptual or avant-garde (*xianfeng*) photography during the 1990s, the role of the photograph or video was at first primarily to record performance works, as with Rong Rong's photographing of events staged by Zhang Huan and others in Beijing's East Village, which were then marketed; subsequently, between 1995 and 1997, this polarity was reversed as artists like Hong Lei and Qiu Zhijie turned to staging events for the sake of photographic experimentation. See Zhu Qi, ed., *1990 nian yilai de Zhongguo xianfeng sheying, Chinese Avant-garde Photography Since 1990* (Changsha: Hunan meishu chubanshe, 2004).

96. Personal conversation, May 1995.

97. Even during the Cultural Revolution, the audience had seen enough real violence in state-arranged public spectacles to preclude such realities making their way onto the screen for the rest of the world to witness — as in the highly stylized *White-Haired Girl* (director Xie Jin, 1972), where the summary execution of the landlord is conducted offstage and confirmed only by the sound of drumbeats replacing gunfire. Extremes of graphic violence were allowed, unusually, in *Red Sorghum* (1987, director Zhang Yimou, cinematographer Gu Changwei) and *Red Cherry* (1995, director Ye Daying, cinematographer Li Zhang), depicting Japanese and Nazi atrocities, respectively, but even these were tame by international standards.

98. Only the angle of the rising dust is wrong, kicked straight up rather than angled away from the victim.

99. Walt Whitman, 1855 Preface to *Leaves of Grass*, in *Walt Whitman, Complete Poetry and Collected Prose* (New York: The Library of America, 1982), 14.

100. Personal communication.

101. Xiao Peng, "'*Guizi zhuang*' de di sige zhenjiao" ("The 'Fourth Stitch' of the Devil's Uniform"), *Da Zhong dianying* (1999.3), 9.

102. Peter Hessler, *Oracle Bones: A Journey Through Time in China* (New York: Harper Collins, 2006), 344.

103. In his article on *In the Heat of the Sun*, Song Weijie quotes Roland Barthes to emphasize the noncontradictory character of these two, myth and falsification: "Myth hides nothing and flaunts nothing: it distorts; myth is neither a lie nor a confession: it is an inflection." Song Weijie, "Transgression, Submission, and the Fantasy of Youth Subculture: The Nostalgic Symptoms of *In the Heat of the Sun*," in Haili Kong and John A. Lent, eds., *100 Years of Chinese Cinema: A Generational Dialogue* (Norwalk, CT: Eastbridge, 2006), 173.

104. *Li Chi* [*Li ji*], *Book of Rites*, trans. James Legge (1885; New Hyde Park, NY: University Books, 1967), 2:229.

105. Eiko Ikegami, *The Taming of the Samurai: Honorific Individualism and the Making of Modern Japan* (Cambridge, MA: Harvard University Press, 1995), 99–101.

106. Ibid., 101.

107. For example, in a famous encounter between the early third-century generals Guan Yu and Pang De, the doomed Pang De urged his soldiers, "The valorous leader fears death less than desertion; the brave warrior does not break faith to save his life! This is the day of my death, but I will fight on to the last." Captured, "Pang De was sent for. He came, pride and anger flashing from his eyes; he did not kneel but stood boldly erect.... 'Rather than surrender to you I would perish beneath the sword,' cried Pang. He reviled his captors without ceasing till, losing patience at last, Guan Yu sent him to his death. He was beheaded. He stretched out his neck for the headsman's sword. Out of pity, he was honourably buried." Luo Guanzhong, attributed, *Romance of the Three Kingdoms*, trans. C.H. Brewitt-Taylor (Rutland, VT: Charles Tuttle, 1959), 2:153–54. A well-known painting by Shang Xi for the early Ming court (now in the Palace Museum collection, Beijing) illustrates Pang De's final resistance, bound and defiant. See Silbergeld, *China Into Film*, 59.

Death rather than capture has also been expected of People's Liberation Army troops. In his National Book Award–winning story of a Korean War prisoner, Ha Jin reports that the Seventh Article of the Code of Conduct of the PLA commands, "Never surrender. Never let yourself be taken prisoner even at the cost of your life." Ha Jin, *War Trash* (New York: Pantheon Books, 2004), 103. (Ha Jin based this assertion on his own five-year's PLA experience; personal communication, June 2005.) Elsewhere in the book, his main character writes, "We all felt ashamed of becoming POWs because we should have died rather than submit to capture. I often heard some men say they had 'smeared soot on Chairman Mao's face.' The guilt weighted

NOTES

heavily on their consciences." On returning to the People's Republic from captivity in Korea, many of these prisoners are made to wish they had died" (235). However, at my request the artist Zhi Lin (see note 137 below) queried his parents about this: his father, as a counterintelligence officer who worked with POWs and his mother as an army nurse, both marched into Korea on November 7, 1950, for the 59th Division of the 20th Army and both received extensive training on how to behave if captured. Both write that they never heard of this Seventh Article and, instead, that they were instructed about not revealing military information in captivity.

108. Asked whether his forthcoming film was particularly concerned with the militant nature of the Japanese, Jiang Wen replied, "I am not interested in the Japanese people, I am interested in people. I just don't understand, looking well at any given person, how he can take up a blade to slaughter another. How can he think that way and why is he like that?" Interview with Feng Mei, *Da Zhong dianying* (1999.3), 4.

109. Yasukuni Jinja ("Peaceful Nation Shrine"), located in Tokyo just outside the Imperial Palace moat, founded in 1869 and given this name in 1879, was dedicated to those "loyal to the emperor" in Japan's "defensive" and "sacred" wars dating back to the Meiji Restoration, an estimated 2.5 million people. In 1978, more than one thousand convicted World War II criminals, including fourteen class A criminals, were secretly enshrined there, most notably War Minister Tojo Hideki, who was executed under Allied supervision in 1948. The enshrinement became public knowledge a year later, and subsequent attempts to have them removed have repeatedly failed. Visits by Japanese prime ministers from 1975 on — on the anniversary

of Japan's August 15 surrender to Allied forces — have become the occasion for protests by the Chinese and South Korean governments, viewed as a violation of the separation of church and state written into Japan's postwar constitution, a bow by official authority to the militarist elements still powerful in Japanese society, and a refusal by the country to come to grips with its flawed history. The September 2005 Osaka High Court ruling that Prime Minister Junichiro Koizumi's "private" visits to the shrine beginning in 2001 were official and an illegal violation of Japan's constitutional separation of church and state did not prevent a visit the next August. More recently, it has been reported that the late emperor Hirohito's own absence from the shrine in his later years was in opposition to the installation there of these fourteen war criminals; Martin Fackler, "Diaries Add Hirohito to Debate On Visits to Japan War Shrine," *New York Times*, July 21, 2006, A11. The shrine includes a military museum dating back to 1872, now housing modern tanks and other military weapons, with installations asserting that America forced the Japanese attack on Pearl Harbor for its own economic purposes and blaming the Chinese commander in Nanjing for the violence that took place there until Japanese troops restored the peace. Jiang Wen visited the Yasukuni Shrine as part of his meticulous preparation for making this film, which provoked reaction and resentment in China as he undoubtedly knew it must; see "Actor's Visit to Japanese Shrine Sparks Spite" at <www.china.org.cn/english/NM-e/36679.htm>, July 8, 2002.

110. The China art historian will be reminded of Xu Bing's performance works *Case Study of Transference*, in which a dominant male pig covered with pseudo-English writing mounts a passive female pig inscribed with pseudo-Chinese characters, 1994, and *Cultural Animals*, 1994, in which the place of the female pig is taken by an inscribed papier-mâché Chinese male. See Erickson, *The Art of Xu Bing*, 59–62.

111. In his personal memoirs, uncompleted at the time of his death in 2005, the late Princeton professor of Chinese history Frederick Mote wrote of his experiences after entering China in May 1945 as a Chinese language interpreter with the Office of Strategic Services. "MacArthur's headquarters in Tokyo repeatedly sent messages to the China Command insisting that evidence of Chinese revenge attacks against the Japanese must be gathered and dispatched to Tokyo immediately, to match the quantities of such material being sent from Korea, French Indochina, and the Philippines. In fact, none of our offices in what had been the Japanese occupied regions could find significant evidence for acts of revenge. Earlier, while still in Nanking in September, Captain Coulson forwarded to our China headquarters a report I prepared for him about the lack of revenge sentiment in Nanking at that time." "Anti-Japanese sentiment," Mote wrote, "had been fostered initially by the call to boycott Japanese businesses and Japanese-made goods during the May Fourth Movement in 1919 and the years thereafter. It remained strong through the war years, as millions of Chinese lost family members and property, and wartime hardships were experienced through all the strata of Chinese society. The surprising thing is that when the war ended, the widely felt resentment toward Japan generated few demands for revenge and very little violent behavior. If anything, the behavior of Soviet troops that invaded Manchuria when Stalin declared war on Japan on August 8, a day after the bombing of Hiroshima, aroused more widespread

resentment." And Mote noted that, "As the peace arrangements were being worked out, Chiang [Kai-shek] demanded the return of some valuable antiquities and works of art plundered from museums, or presented to the Japanese by leaders of the three puppet governments (in Manchuria, in Peking, and in Nanking), but he announced that the attitude of the Chinese government toward the defeated Japanese would be to 'recompense injury with kindness.' His stance troubled some Chinese, and mystified many others. His motives were no doubt very complex." On a more personal note, Mote recalled a conversation he had, shortly after the war's end, with a victim of the 1937 Nanjing massacre who had survived but nonetheless lost a leg: "I looked out from his open shopdoor to the small grassy circle, trying to imagine the event, when a small, elderly Japanese lady, in a drab kimono, with a *furoshiki* in which she carried the few items of groceries she had purchased, walked past his door. I said: 'Aren't you angry at these Japanese people still walking the streets of Nanking. See those Japanese soldiers over there? They are now being disarmed, but they still walk freely on the streets. Wouldn't you like at least to throw a rock at them?' He hesitated to reply to my disturbing question. But eventually, slowly and calmly, pointing to the little old [Japanese] grandmother, he said he had no reason to blame her for the violence in 1937. As for the soldiers, he said they were not the ones who eight years ago had killed so many people. Those had all been sent on to other war fronts in the years that followed, and probably most of them were dead by now. In short, he had no cause for revenge against these soldiers now on the scene. Perhaps his attitudes were unusual, but I found virtually no one who sought revenge, despite deep feelings of resentment that many shared." From chapter one, "Getting There," unpaginated, in Frederick Mote, *China and the Vocation of History in the Twentieth Century: A Personal Memoir* (Princeton: East Asia Library Journal and Princeton University Press, forthcoming).

112. Lu Xun, *Diary of a Madman and Other Stories*, trans. William A. Lyell (Honolulu: University of Hawai'i Press, 1990).

113. The distinction between demonization and animalization deserves some further study. What predominates here, however, is the Japanese characterization of Chinese as animals and the Chinese regard of Japanese as devils ("ghosts" really, *guizi*). At one point in the film, a Japanese soldier even advises another, "Act like a *guizi* and frighten them." In her book *The Origin of Satan*, Elaine Pagels's main thesis is that "this greatest and most dangerous enemy did not originate, as one might expect, as an outsider, an alien, or a stranger. Satan is not the distant enemy but the intimate enemy—one's trusted colleague, close associate, brother." Early Christian demonization was directed not against Romans or Syrians but Jews, their fellow Palestineans. "Those [Christians] who asked, 'How could God's own angel become his enemy?' were thus asking, in effect, 'How could one of *us* become one of *them*?'" Elaine Pagels, *The Origin of Satan* (New York: Vintage, 1996), 49. Here, things are not quite as clear or consistent, and there is a distinction between Chinese ghosts and the biblical Devil, but there may be something more logical to this than the mere Chinese habit of referring to any outsiders as "foreign ghosts" or "foreign devils" (*yang guizi*). Japanese determination to reverse sixteen centuries of Chinese cultural dominance and impose their own hegemony upon the rest of Asia presents the Chinese as a once-

lofty people grown corrupt and lazy and fallen, in a karmic way, to the level of mere beasts; while in Chinese eyes, this historical reversal is viewed as a betrayal by once-loyal (or subordinate, at least) Japanese, now ghosts or lost souls.

114. The word for ant (*yi*) was conventionally used in China by the humble petitioner (as "I" or "we"), so the identification of Ma Dasan with the solitary ant that is flicked away lends another level of resonance to the detail.

115. Silbergeld, "In Praise of Government"; Robert E. Harrist, *Power and Virtue: The Horse in Chinese Art* (New York: China Institute in America, 1997).

116. The detail is from *Two Horses, Fat and Lean* by Ren Renfa. The artist's inscription makes it clear that the function of the two horses is to represent the two kinds of motives by which one may choose to serve or not serve the Yuan Mongol government, either selfish or selfless, and that one may not readily know any given scholar's motives simply by judging surface appearances. For a translation of this inscription, see Silbergeld, "In Praise of Government," 170, n26; this article interprets about a painting in which five horses come to justify the Mongol suppression of a mid-fourteenth century Chinese uprising.

117. Sima Qian, *Records of the Grand Historian of China,* trans. Burton Watson (New York: Columbia University Press, 1961), 1:52. In Western literature, the stigmatization of people as animals can be traced at least as far back as Ishmael in the Bible, Abraham's son and, in Jewish and Islamic tradition, the progenitor of the Arabian peoples, but described by an angel of the Lord as "a wild ass of a man; His hand against everyone, And everyone's hand against him." Genesis 16:12–14, *Tanakh: The Holy Scriptures* (Philadelphia and Jerusalem: Jewish Publication Society, 1985), 23.

118. Because of the Chinese concern for bodily integrity, death by starvation, while slow and painful but typically ending prematurely in strangulation within the constraining stocks, was favored over quicker methods that desecrated the body. For the more torturous methods, a massive amount of alcohol or opium was traditionally administered to help ease the suffering.

119. Hegel may have been wrong in detail and degree but not in essence when he remarked that in China, "punishments are generally corporal chastisements. Among us, this would be an insult to honor; not so in China…. If a son complains of injustice done to him by his father, or a younger brother by an elder, he receives a hundred blows with a bamboo, and is banished for three years, *if he is in the right*; if not, he is strangled." Georg Wilhelm Friedrich Hegel, *The Philosophy of History* (posth. 1837; New York: Dover, 1956), 128–29. In modern times, the Chinese government first authorized execution by lethal injection in 1997 and first carried it out in 1998; while also continuing to practice death by the bullet, in 2003 they instituted a fleet of darkened-window mobile lethal-injection minivans, helping to take most of China's 3,400-plus executions per year out of the public eye even in rural China. ("China is wary enough about its death penalty system that it has long designated its number of executions as a state secret. A hint at the number came last year when a high-level delegate to the National People's Congress publicly estimated that it was 'nearly 10,000.' In 2004, Amnesty International documented at least 3,400 executions—out of 3,797 worldwide that year—but cautioned that China's number was probably far higher. Outside scholars have put the annual number as high as 15,000." Jim Yardley, "In Worker's Death, View of China's Harsh Justice," *New York Times*, December 31, 2005, A9.

120. From the *Xiao Jing, The Book of Filial Piety*; cf. *The Sacred Books of China: The Texts of Confucianism* , Vol. I, *The Hsiao King*, trans. James Legge (Oxford: Clarendon Press, 1899), 481. This passage is illustrated in a handscroll attributed to the eleventh-century painter Li Gonglin, reproduced in Richard Barnhart et al., *Li Gonglin's Classic of Filial Piety* (New York: The Metropolitan Museum of Art, 1993), 138–39, with discussion on 122–23. For a review of early-twentieth-century fiction related to the topic, see David Der-wei Wang, *The Monster That Is History: History Violence, and Fictional Writing in Twentieth-Century China* (Berkeley and Los Angeles: University of California Press, 2004).

Chinese justice is not famous for its mercy. The defendant is presumed guilty or the government would not be bringing the case. The modern, Communist Chinese standard is "Leniency to those who confess, severity to those who refuse." But a study of Chinese justice, punishment, and mercy by Brian McKnight describes a more benign traditional attitude: "In our earliest written references to the problems of punishment and forgiveness the Zhou founder King Wu speaks to his younger brother about the propriety of dealing leniently with those guilty even of great crimes, provided they were committed through mishap or inadvertence. For the deliberate malefactor the penalty should be death without pardon. Strict and implacable justice to those deliberately guilty with knowledge aforethought no matter how minor their offense, full and complete pardon for those guilty through mishap or mistake no matter how grave the crime—this became the main doctrine on judicial grace." The author continues, in a historical vein, "First enunciated by King Wu, it remained current doctrine and was reaffirmed in the late, forged sections of the *Book of Documents*. Given in an epigram in the 'Counsels of the Great Yu,' it was spelled out at greater length in the 'Canon of Shun,' where it was said that Shun 'gave delineation of the statutory punishments, enacting banishment as a mitigation (*yu*) of the Five Great Inflictions [*wu xing*]." Brian McKnight, *The Quality of Mercy: Amnesties and Traditional Chinese Justice* (Honolulu: University of Hawaii Press, 1981), 2. For the *Book of Documents* passages, see James Legge, *The Chinese Classics, Vol. 3: The Shoo King* [*Shu jing*] (1865; Hong Kong: Hong Kong University Press, 1960), 388 ff. and 38 ff., respectively.

121. Endymion Wilkinson, *Chinese History: A Manual* (Cambridge, MA: Harvard University Asia Center for the Harvard-Yenching Institute, and Harvard University Press, 2000), 724.

122. Ibid., 725, 726. Wilkinson offers a list of some of "the most popular derogative terms from all periods of Chinese history" (726).

123. Illustrated with text in Wang Qi, ed., *Sancai tuhui* (1607; Taipei: Chengwen chubanshe, 1970), *juan* 13:25. Much of the *Sancai tuhui* material on this subject was derived from Hu Wenhuan et al., eds., *Xin ke luochong lu* (1593; Beijing: Xueyuan chubanshe, 2001). See also the illustrated translation of *Shan Hai Ching: Legendary Geography and Wonders of Ancient China*, trans. Hsiao-Chieh Cheng et al. (Taipei: National Institute for Compilation and Translation, 1985); Richard J. Smith, *Chinese Maps: Images of "All Under Heaven"* (New York: Oxford University Press, 1996), 16–22.

124. Stylistically and compositionally diverse versions of this painting are in the Palace Museum, Beijing; the Yunnan Provincial Museum, Kunming (two paintings);

the Freer Gallery of Art, Smithsonian Institution, Washington, DC; the Princeton University Art Museum; the University of California, Berkeley, Art Museum; and the Steven Junkunc collection, Chicago. See Thomas Lawton, *Chinese Figure Painting* (Washington, DC: Freer Gallery of Art, Smithsonian Institution, 1973), 152–55; Kiyohiko Munakata, *Sacred Mountains in Chinese Art* (Urbana: Krannert Art Museum; Champaign: University of Illinois Press, 1991), 105–10; Pao-chen Ch'en, catalogue entry in Wen Fong et al., *Images of the Mind: Selections from the Edward L. Elliott Family and John B. Elliott Collections of Chinese Calligraphy and Painting at The Art Museum, Princeton University* (Princeton: The Art Museum, Princeton University, 1984), 323–30.

125. Cf. Nishijima Sadao, in Denis Twitchett and Michael Loewe, eds., *The Cambridge History of China, Vol. 1: The Ch'in and Han Empires, 221 B.C.–A.D. 220* (New York: Cambridge University Press, 1986), 554.

126. Richard Von Glahn, *The Sinister Way: The Divine and the Demonic in Chinese Religious Culture* (Berkeley and Los Angeles: University of California Press, 2004), 78–80; Robert Campany, *Strange Writing: Anomaly Accounts in Early Medieval China* (Albany: State University of New York Press, 1996), 106.

127. "Racial discourse [in twentieth-century China] thrived largely thanks to, and not in spite of, folk models of identity, based on patrilineal descent and common stock. Instead of crude generalisations about the role of 'the state' in the deployment of racial categories which would have been disseminated from top to bottom, or the popular 'cloud to dust' theory of cultural change, a degree of circularity, or reciprocal interaction, between popular culture and officially sponsored discourses of race has been proposed." Frank Dikötter, "Racial Discourse in China: Continuities and

Permutations," in Dikötter, *The Construction of Racial Identities in China and Japan* (Hong Kong: Hong Kong University Press, 1997), 32–33. See also Frank Dikötter, *The Discourse of Race in Modern China* (London: C. Hurst; Stanford: Stanford University Press; Hong Kong: Hong Kong University Press, 1992).

128. Dikötter, *Construction*, 22.

129. Ibid., 21, from a 1921 primary school textbook.

130. Ibid., 2.

131. Ibid., 19.

132. Albert Bandura devised a now-classic experiment at Stanford University in which electric shocks were supposedly delivered as punishment for bad performance to a group of college students by three other groups of college students. When one of the groups delivering the shocks was allowed to "accidentally" overhear an experimenter's single offhand remark that those to be punished "seem like animals" or were "an animalistic, rotten bunch," the severity of punishment "delivered" by that group was significantly higher than that delivered by the other groups which heard either positive or no references at all to the shock "victims's" character. A. Bandura, B. Underwood, and M.E. Fromson, "Disinhibition of Aggression Through Diffusion of Responsibility and Dehumanization of Victims," *Journal of Research in Personality* 9.4 (1975), 253–69. See also V.W. Bernard, P. Ottenberg, and F. Redl, "Dehumanization: A Composite Psychological Defense in Relation to Modern War," in R. Perrucci and M. Pilisuck, eds., *The Psychological Basis of Practice* (New York: Harper and Row, 1963).

133. Anne Thurston, "Urban Violence during the Cultural Revolution: Who Is to Blame?," in Jonathan Lipman and Stevan Harrell, eds., *Violence in China: Essays in Culture and Counterculture* (Albany: State University of New York Press, 1990), 159. See also the online "working paper" by Jeffrey Wasserstrom and Sin-kiong Wong, "Taunting the Turtles and Damning the Dogs: Animal Epithets and Political Conflict in Modern China" <www.indiana.edu/~easc/resources/working_paper/noframe_9b_taunt.htm>.

134. In his own account of this, Lu Xun wrote, "In those days [while at Sendai Medical College in Tokyo], we were shown lantern slides of microbes; and if the lecture ended early, the instructor might show slides of natural scenery or news to fill up the time. Since this was during the Russo-Japanese War, there were many war slides, and I had to join in the clapping and cheering in the lecture hall along with the other students. It was a long time since I had seen any compatriots, but one day I saw a news-reel slide of a number of Chinese, one of them bound and the rest standing around him. They were all sturdy fellows but appeared completely apathetic. According to the commentary, the one with his hands bound was a spy working for the Russians who was to be beheaded by the Japanese military as a warning to others, while the Chinese beside him had come to enjoy the spectacle. Before the term was over I had left for Tokyo, because this slide convinced me that medical science was not so important after all. The people of a weak and backward country, however strong and healthy they might be, could only serve to be made examples of or as witnesses of such futile spectacles; and it was not necessarily deplorable if many of them died of illness. The most important thing, therefore, was to change their spirit; and since at that time I felt that literature was the best means to this end, I decided to promote a literary movement." Lu Xun, Preface to *Call to Arms* (*Nahan*), in Lu Xun, *Lu Xun, Selected Works*, trans. Yang Xianyi and Gladys Yang (Beijing: Foreign Languages Press, 1980), 1:34–35.

135. David Der-Wei Wang, *The Monster That Is History*, 35.

136. Zhi Lin's "five punishments" include *Flaying* (1993), *Decapitation* (1995), *Firing Squad* (1996), *Starvation* (1999) and *Drawing and Quartering* (2003). The last of these was completed as a finished drawing in charcoal; a painted version of this, now in the Frye Art Museum, Seattle, was completed in 2007. See Jan Schall et al., *Zhi Lin: Crossing History / Crossing Cultures* (Terre Haute: University of Indiana; Seattle: Frye Art Museum; Los Angeles: Koplin Del Rio Gallery, 2003). Born in 1959 in Nanjing and now a professor at the University of Washington, Seattle, Zhi Lin trained as a printmaker at the National Academy in Hangzhou and first came West in 1987. He was in the second of his three M.F.A. degree programs at the Slade School of Fine Art at the University of London in 1989 when events at Tiananmen convinced him that "art is not only for beauty and personal preference, but necessary for social change." Across the surface of each painted version is silkscreened in pale shades the silhouette of an ancient bronze ritual trident, a weapon symbolizing rule by force, four-to-five feet tall in the original examples archaeologically excavated from royal tombs of the Zhongshan state, including that of King Cuo (d. c. 308 BCE); they are intended here as a subliminal message of the power of external authority, but the artist has depicted them in reserve, lightly coloring the ground surrounding them rather than printing the bronze figures themselves, and effectively removing them from the scene in an anti-authoritarian gesture. Zhi Lin's works are bordered by stenciled depictions of Confucius, Laozi and Zhuangzi, Guanyin, Sun Yat-sen and Mao

Zedong, while the mountings are those of a Tibetan thanka, in reference to the Dalai Lama.

137. For photo-essays on the public exercise of justice during the Cultural Revolution, including a campaign leading to public executions at Harbin, August–September 1967, see Li Zhensheng, *Red-Color News Soldier*, 186–200.

138. See Philip P. Choy, Lorraine Dong, and Marion K. Hom, eds., *The Coming Man: 19th-Century American Perceptions of the Chinese* (Seattle: University of Washington Press, 1994), pl. 75, "Darwin's Theory Illustrated—The Creation of Chinaman and Pig," from *The Wasp*, January 6, 1877, 217, which depicts Chinese as pigs descended from monkeys, and pl. 86, "The Chinese Invasion," from *Puck*, n.d., in which Chinese swimming to American shores are likened to rats. See also Jean Pfaelzer, *Driven Out: The Forgotten War Against Chinese Americans* (New York: Random House, 2007).

139. Chen Chieh-jen, in Nedoma and Chang, *A Strange Heaven*, 32–34. See there, the two historical photographs composited for this image. See also Chen Chieh-jen's video *Lingchi*, 2002, a digital "recreation" of a public flaying, based on a 1905 French photograph.

140. William Golding, *Lord of the Flies* (New York: Capricorn Books, 1959), 189.

141. Jiang Wen, interview with Tony Rayns. The Chinese government has frequently used the historical lesson that "backwardness invites aggression" (*luohuo jiuyao aida*) in support of its current drive for economic development.

142. "A 2000 film by one of China's leading directors, Jiang Wen, remains banned because it depicted friendliness between a captured Japanese soldier and Chinese villagers. Although the film showed plenty of brutality, censors ruled that *Devils at the*

Doorstep gave viewers 'the impression that Chinese civilians neither hated nor resisted Japanese invaders.'" Matthew Forney, "Why China Loves to Hate Japan," *Time Magazine*, December 10, 2005, <www.time.com/time/world/article/0,8599,1139759,00.html>.

143. *Time Asia* argues for irrelevancy: "The Film Bureau in Beijing is slated to be dismantled as the state bureaucracy is streamlined; some film people believe that, by stoking this controversy, the censors are trying to make themselves appear indispensible. 'It seems I am caught in a political power play,' Jiang says." Richard Corliss, "Devils on his Doorstep," *Time Asia Magazine* 156.3, July 24, 2000, <www.time.com/time/asia/magazine/2000/0724/china.jiangwen.html>.

144. Ibid.

145. Hessler, *Oracle Bones*, 346–47.

146. Ibid., 346.

147. *Xin Zhongguo waijiao yu lingshi gongzuo* (Beijing: Dangdai Zhongguo chubanshe, 1987), *ziliao* 3, 127–28; *Mao Zedong de guoji jiaowang* (Beijing: Zhonggong dangshi chubanshe, 1995), 41; cited in Geremie R. Barmé, "Mirrors on History on a Sino-Japanese Moment and Some Antecedents," *Japan Focus* online journal, May 16, 2005, article 272 <japanfocus.org/products/details/1713>.

148. Zimbardo, *The Lucifer Effect*, 212.

149. In Jane Elliott's well-known experiment with her third-grade students in Riceville, Iowa, she assigned those with blue eyes a favored relationship with their brown-eyed peers and the favored students promptly assumed a dominant role, quickly achieving higher test scores and even abusing their "inferiors" both verbally and physically, to which the brown-eyed students readily acquiesced. After Elliott told her class she had "erred" and reversed the privilege, the brown-eyes quickly began to achieve the higher test scores while the blue-eyed students regressed, and the newly dominant students quickly began to discriminate against and abuse their former abusers. William Peters, *A Class Divided: Then and Now* (New Haven, CT: Yale University Press, 1985).

150. Zimbardo, *The Lucifer Effect*, 187.

151. Ibid., 213.

152. Ibid., xiii.

153. Cf. Hannah Arendt, *Eichman in Jerusalem: A Report on the Banality of Evil* (1963; New York: Penguin Classics, 2006). In his introduction to this edition, Amos Elon writes that "the Israeli court psychiatrist who examined [Adolph] Eichman found him a 'Completely normal man, more normal, at any rate, than I am after examining him,' the implication being that the coexistence of normality and bottomless cruelty explodes our ordinary conceptions and presents the true enigma [of human character put on trial in the Eichman case]" (xv, 25).

154. Zimbardo, *The Lucifer Effect*, 197, 181.

155. Ibid., 212, 211–12.

156. Daqing Yang, "The Challenges of the Nanjing Massacre: Reflections on Historical Inquiry," in Joshua A. Fogel, ed. *The Nanjing Massacre in History and Historiography* (Berkeley and Los Angeles: University of California Press, 2000), 157–58. Yang quotes Charles Maier's *The Unmasterable Past: History, Holocaust, and German Natiional Identity* (Cambridge, MA: Harvard University Press, 1988), 14.

157. Ma Dasan parallels Zimbardo's "prisoner" 8612, who was both the first to rebel and, failing in that, the first to break down and be released from the experiment. See ibid., 209.

158. For a discussion of this beheading in the context of Lu Xun's writings, see Gary G. Xu, *Sinascape: Contemporary Chinese Cinema* (Lanham, MD: Rowman and Littlefield, 2007), 51–54.

159. Michael Sullivan, *Art and Artists of Twentieth-Century China* (Berkeley and Los Angeles: University of California Press, 1996), 71; for the finished 1940 version, see pl. 7.4.

160. Mao Zedong, speech delivered on June 11, 1945 (after the fall of Germany and before the Japanese surrender) at the conclusion of the Seventh National Congress of the Communist Party, from *The Selected Works of Mao Tse-tung* (Beijing: Foreign Languages Press, 1967), 3:271–74.

161. In current Party rhetoric, these two historical claims have been triangulated with the "opening up" to capital formation of China since 1979 to represent the "three major undertakings" of the Party in establishing its role as "vanguard" of the working class and maintaining its "progressive" character. Cf. Chairman Hu Jintao's national television address, on June 31, 2006, celebrating the 85th anniversary of the establishment of the Chinese Communist Party.

162. The historian can trace such accusations of structural inequity back to the talented writer Wang Shiwei, whose essay "Wild Lillies" was published at Yan'an in *Liberation Daily* in March 1942: "Some say there is no system of hierarchy and privilege in Yan'an. This is not true. It exists. Others say, yes, there is, but it is justified. This requires us to think with our heads.... I am no egalitarian. But I do not think it is necessary or justified to have multiple grades in food or clothing." Chang and Halliday, *Mao: The Unknown Story*, 242. Mao had Wang imprisoned, and when the Communists left Yan'an, Wang was executed and his body thrown into a well.

163. Even at Yan'an, the unofficial formula for Communist military effort had been "70 per cent expanding our own forces, 20 per cent resisting the Guomindang and 10 per cent fighting Japan." Philip Short, *Mao: A Life* (New York: Henry Holt, 2000), 408.

Bibliography

Addiss, Stephen, et al. *Japanese Ghosts and Demons: Art of the Supernatural*. New York: George Braziller, 1985.

Agee, James. *Agee on Film: Reviews and Comments by James Agee*. New York: Beacon, 1985.

Arendt, Hannah. *Eichman in Jerusalem: A Report on the Banality of Evil*. New York: Penguin Books, 2006. (Originally published 1963.)

Bandura, A., B. Underwood, and M.E. Fromson. "Disinhibition of Aggression Through Diffusion of Responsibility and Dehumanization of Victims." *Journal of Research in Personality*, 9.4 (1975), 253–269.

Barmé, Geremie. *In the Red: On Contemporary Chinese Culture*. New York: Columbia University Press, 1999.

———. "Mirrors on History on a Sino-Japanese Moment and Some Antecedents." *Japan Focus* online journal, May 16, 2005, article 272 <japanfocus.org/products/details/1713>.

———. *Shades of Mao: The Posthumous Cult of the Great Leader*. Armonk, NY: M.E. Sharpe, 1996.

———. "Wang Shuo and Hooligan ('Liumang') Culture." *Australian Journal of Chinese Affairs* 28 (July 1992), 23–64.

Bennett, Brian. "Back in Action." Interview with Jiang Wen. *Time Asia Magazine* 159.24, June 24, 2002 <www.time.com/time/asia/magazine/printout/0,13675,501020624-263045,00.html>, 3.

Braester, Yomi. *Witness Against History: Literature, Film, and Public Discourse in Twentieth-Century China*. Stanford: Stanford University Press, 2003.

Cartier-Bresson, Henri. *Henri Cartier-Bresson*. New York: Aperture, 1987.

Chan, Anita. *Children of Mao: Personality Development and Political Activism in the Red Guard Generation*. Seattle: University of Washington Press, 1985.

Chang, Jung, and Jon Halliday. *Mao: The Unknown Story*. New York: Alfred A. Knopf, 2005.

Chen Xiaomei. "Growing Up With Posters in the Maoist Era." In Harriet Evans and Stephanie Donald, eds., *Picturing Power in the People's Republic of China: Posters of the Cultural Revolution*, 101–122. Lanham, MD: Rowman and Littlefield, 1999.

Choy, Philip P., Lorraine Dong, and Marion Hom, eds. *The Coming Man: 19th-Century American Perceptions of the Chinese*. Seattle: University of Washington Press, 1994.

Cui, Shuqin. "Working From the Margins: Urban Cinema and Independent Directors in Contemporary China." In Sheldon Lu and Emelie Yueh-yu Yeh, eds. *Chinese Language Film: Historiography, Poetics, Politics*, 96–119. Honolulu: University of Hawai'i Press, 2005.

Corliss, Richard. "Devils on his Doorstep." *Time Asia Magazine* 156.3, July 24, 2000, <www.time.com/time/asia/magazine/2000/0724/china.jiangwen.html>.

BIBLIOGRAPHY

Corneille, Pierre. *The Theatre of Illusion*. Translated by Richard Wilbur. Orlando, FL: Harcourt, 2007.

Dikötter, Frank. *Crime, Punishment, and the Prison in Modern China*. New York: Columbia University Press, 2002.

Dikötter, Frank, ed. *The Construction of Racial Identities in China and Japan*. Hong Kong: Hong Kong University Press, 1997.

Erickson, Britta. *The Art of Xu Bing: Words Without Meaning, Meaning Without Words*. Washington, D.C.: Arthur M. Sackler Gallery, Smithsonian Institution; Seattle: University of Washington Press, 2001.

Evans, Harriet, and Stephanie Donald, eds. *Picturing Power in the People's Republic of China: Posters of the Cultural Revolution*. Lanham, MD: Rowman and Littlefield, 1999.

Faber, John. *Great News Photos and the Stories behind Them*. New York: Dover Books, 1978.

Fraser, Stewart E., comp. *100 Great Chinese Posters: Recent Examples of "The People's Art" from the People's Republic of China*. New York: Images Graphiques, 1977.

Gao Minglu, ed. *Inside Out: New Chinese Art*. San Francisco: San Francisco Museum of Modern Art; New York: Asia Society Galleries; Berkeley and Los Angeles: University of California Press, 1998.

Golding, William. *Lord of the Flies*. New York: Capricorn Books, 1959.

Graves, Robert. *I, Claudius: From the Autobiography of Tiberius Claudius, Born B.C. X, Murdered and Deified A.D. LIV*. New York: Random House, 1961.

Ha Jin [Jin Xuefei]. *War Trash*. New York: Pantheon Books, 2004.

Harrist, Robert E. *Power and Virtue: The Horse in Chinese Art*. New York: China Institute in America, 1997.

Hay, John. *Kernels of Energy, Bones of Earth: The Rock in Chinese Art*. New York: China Institute in America, 1985.

——. "Values and History in Chinese Painting: Hsieh Ho Revisited and The Hierarchic Evolution of Structure." *Res* 6 (Fall 1983), 73–111, and *Res* 7/8 (Spring/Autumn 1984), 102–136.

Hessler, Peter. *Oracle Bones: A Journey Through Time in China*. New York: Harper Collins/Harper Perennial, 2007.

Hu Wenhuan et al., eds. *Xin ke luochong lu*. Beijing: Xueyuan chubanshe, 2001. (Originally published 1593.)

Hu Zhichuan et al., eds. *Zhongguo sheying shi: 1840–1937* (*A History of Chinese Photography: 1840–1937*). Beijing: Zhongguo sheying chubanshe, 1987.

Hyman, Ira E., and Elizabeth F. Loftus. "Errors in Autobiographical Memory." *Clinical Psychology Review* 18.8 (December 1998), 933–947.

Ikegami, Eiko. *The Taming of the Samurai: Honorific Individualism and the Making of Modern Japan*. Cambridge, MA: Harvard University Press, 1995.

Jiang Wen et al. *Yibu dianying de dansheng* (*The Birth of a Film*). Beijing: Huayi chubanshe, 1997.

Kamen, Paula. *Finding Iris Chang: Friendship, Ambition, and the Loss of an Extraordinary Mind*. Philadelphia: Da Capo Press, 2007.

Kent, Richard K. "Fine Art Amateur Photography in Republican-Period Shanghai." In Jerome Silbergeld, Dora C.Y. Ching, Alfreda Murck, and Judith G. Smith, eds., *Bridges to Heaven: Essays on East Asian Art in Honor of Professor Wen C. Fong*. Princeton: Princeton University Press, forthcoming.

King, David. *The Commissar Vanishes: The Falsification of Photographs and Art in Stalin's Russia*. New York: Metropolitan Books/Henry Holt and Company, 1997.

Li Chi, Book of Rites. Translated by James Legge. New Hyde Park, NY: University Books, 1967.

Li Zhensheng. *Red-Color News Soldier*. London and New York: Phaidon, 2003.

Li Zhisui. *The Private Life of Chairman Mao: The Memoirs of Mao's Personal Physician*. Translated by Dai Hongzhao with Anne F. Thurston. Armonk, NY: M.E. Sharpe, 1996.

Liu, Cary. "Chinese Architectural Aesthetics: Patterns of Living and Being between Past and Present." In Ronald Knapp and Kai-yin Lo, eds., *House Home Family: Living and Being Chinese*, 139–159. Honolulu: University of Hawai'i Press, 2005.

Loftus, Elizabeth F. "Memory and Its Distortions." In Alan G. Kraut, ed., *The G. Stanley Hall Lecture Series*, *Volume 2*, 123–154. Washington, D.C.: American Psychological Association, 1982.

Lu, Tonglin. "Fantasy and Ideology in a Chinese Film: A Žižekian Reading of the Cultural Revolution." *Positions* 12.2 (Fall 2004), 539–564.

Lu Xun. *Diary of a Madman and Other Stories*. Translated by William A. Lyell. Honolulu: University of Hawai'i Press, 1990.

———. Preface to *Call to Arms* (*Nahan*). (Originally published 1922.) In Lu Xun, *Lu Xun, Selected Works*. Translated by Yang Xianyi and Gladys Yang, 1:33–38. Beijing: Foreign Languages Press, 1980.

Mao Zedong. *The Selected Works of Mao Tse-tung,* volume 3. Beijing: Foreign Languages Press, 1967.

McKnight, Brian. *The Quality of Mercy: Amnesties and Traditional Chinese Justice*. Honolulu: University Press of Hawaii, 1981.

Molière, Jean Baptiste Poquelin de. *The Misanthrope and Tartuffe*. Translated by Richard Wilbur. Orlando, FL: Harcourt, 1965.

Moorman, Margaret. "Leo Steinberg and the Sexuality of Christ." *Art News* 85.3 (March 1985), 76–85.

Mora, Gilles, ed. *Edward Weston: Forms of Passion*. New York: Harry N. Abrams, 1995.

Mote, Frederick. *China and the Vocation of History in the Twentieth Century: A Personal Memoir*. Princeton: East Asian Library Journal and Princeton University Press, forthcoming.

Nedoma, Petr, and Chang Tsong-zung. *A Strange Heaven: Contemporary Chinese Photography*. Hong Kong: Asia Art Archive, 2003.

Niderst, Alain, ed. *Pierre Corneille: Théâtre* Complet, 3 tomes, 6 vols. Rouen: L'Université de Rouen, 1984.

Orwell, George. *Animal Farm*. New York: Harcourt Brace Jovanovich, 1946.

Pagels, Elaine. *The Origin of Satan*. New York: Vintage, 1996.

Pfaelzer, Jean. *Driven Out: The Forgotten War Against Chinese Americans*. New York: Random House, 2007.

Pickowicz, Paul F., and Yingjin Zhang, eds. *From Underground to Independent: Alternative Film Culture in Contemporary China*. Lanham, MD: Rowman and Littlefield, 2007.

Qu Yuan. "The Nine Songs." In Arthur Waley, translator, *The Nine Songs: A Study in Shamanism in Ancient China*. London: G. Allen and Unwin, 1955.

Rhodes, Gary D., and John Parris Springer, eds. *Docufictions: Essays on the Intersection of Documentary and Fictional Filmmaking*. Jefferson, NC, and London: McFarland and Company, 2006.

Roscoe, Jane, and Craig Hight. *Faking It: Mock-documentary and the Subversion of Factuality*. Manchester and New York: Manchester University Press, 2001.

The Sacred Books of China: The Texts of Confucianism I, The Hsiao King. Translated by James Legge. Oxford: Clarendon Press, 1899.

Schall, Jan, et al. *Zhi Lin: Crossing History/Crossing Cultures*. Terre Haute: University of Indiana; Seattle: Frye Art Museum; Los Angeles: Koplin Del Rio Gallery, 2003.

Schram, Stuart. *Mao Tse-tung*. New York: Simon and Schuster, 1966.

Shan Hai Ching: Legendary Geography and Wonders of Ancient China. Translated by Hsiao-Chieh Cheng et al. Taipei: National Institute for Compilation and Translation, 1985.

Shepard, R.N. "Recognition Memory for Words, Sentences, and Pictures." *Journal of Verbal Learning and Verbal Behavior* 6 (1967), 156–163.

Short, Philip. *Mao: A Life*. New York: Henry Holt, 1999.

Silbergeld, Jerome. *China Into Film: Frames of Reference in Contemporary Chinese Cinema*. London: Reaktion Books, 1999.

——. *Hitchcock with a Chinese Face: Cinematic Doubles, Oedipal Triangles, and China's Moral Voice*. Seattle and London: University of Washington Press, 2004.

——. "In Praise of Government: Chao Yung's Painting, *Noble Steeds*, and Late Yüan Politics." *Artibus Asiae* 46.3 (1985), 159–202.

——. "The Photograph in the Movie: On the Boundaries of Cinematography, Photography, and Videography." In Jerome Silbergeld, Dora C.Y. Ching, Alfreda Murck, and Judith G. Smith, eds., *Bridges to Heaven: Essays on East Asian Art in Honor of Wen C. Fong*. Princeton: Princeton University Press, forthcoming.

Smith, Karen. *Nine Lives: The Birth of Avant-Garde Art in China*. Zurich: Scalo, 2005.

Song, Weijie. "Transgression, Submission, and the Fantasy of Youth Subculture: The Nostalgic Symptoms of *In the Heat of the Sun*." In Haili Kong and John A. Lent, eds., *100 Years of Chinese Cinema: A Generational Dialogue*, 171–182. Norwalk CT: Eastbridge, 2006.

Sontag, Susan. *On Photography*. New York: Farrar, Straus, and Giroux, 1977.

Steinberg, Leo. *The Sexuality of Christ in Renaissance Art and in Modern Oblivion.* 2nd edition, revised; Chicago: University of Chicago Press, 1993.

Sullivan, Michael. *Art and Artists of Twentieth-Century China.* Berkeley and Los Angeles: University of California Press, 1996.

Thom, Ian M. *Andy Warhol: Images.* Vancouver, BC: Douglas & McIntyre, 1995.

Thurston, Anne. "Urban Violence During the Cultural Revolution: Who Is to Blame?" In Jonathan Lipman and Stevan Harrell, eds., *Violence in China: Essays in Culture and Counterculture,* 149–174. Albany: State University of New York Press, 1990.

von Glahn, Richard. *The Sinister Way: The Divine and the Demonic in Chinese Religious Culture.* Berkeley and Los Angeles: University of California Press, 2004.

Wang, David Der-wei. *The Monster that Is History: History, Violence, and Fictional Writing in Twentieth-Century China.* Berkeley and Los Angeles: University of California Press, 2004.

Wang Huangsheng and Hu Wugong, eds. *Zhongguo renben, jishi zai dangdai: Humanism in China, A Contemporary Record of Photography.* Guangzhou: Lingnan meishu chubanshe, 2003.

Wang Qi, ed. *Sancai tuhui.* Taipei: Chengwen chubanshe, 1970. (Originally published 1607.)

Wang Shuo. *Dongwu xiongmeng (Wild Beasts). Shouhuo* 1992.6 (1991), 130–169. Also published, Hong Kong: Chuangjian chuban youxian gongsi, 1994; Beijing: Taihai chubanshe, 2001.

———. "*Yangguang canlan de rizi* zhuiyi." In Jiang Wen et al., *Yibu dianying de dansheng (The Birth of a Film),* 130–169. Beijing: Huayi chubanshe, 1997.

Wei Xidi. "*Jiang Wen zhangdale*" ("Jiang Wen Matures"). <www.filmsea.com.cn/ celebrity_review/200112071223.htm>, dated December 7, 2000.

Weston, Edward. *The Daybooks of Edward Weston, I: Mexico.* Edited by Nancy Newhall. New York: Aperture Books, 1973. (Originally published 1961.)

Wilkinson, Endymion. *Chinese History: A Manual* .Cambridge, MA: Harvard University Asia Center for the Harvard-Yenching Institute, and Harvard University Press, 2000.

Wu Hung. *The Double Screen: Medium and Representation in Chinese Painting.* Chicago: University of Chicago Press, 1996.

Wu Hung and Christopher Phillips. *Between Past and Future: New Photography and Video from China.* Chicago: Smart Museum of Art, University of Chicago; New York: International Center of Photography; Göttigen: Steidl Publishers, 2004.

Wu Hung and Katherine R. Tsiang, eds. *Body and Face in Chinese Visual Culture.* Cambridge, MA: Harvard University Asia Center and Harvard University Press, 2005.

Xiao Peng, "'*Guizi zhuang*' de di sige zhenjiao" ("The Fourth Stitch of the 'Devil's Uniform'"). *Da Zhong dianying* (1999.3), 8–9.

Xu, Gary. *Sinascape: Contemporary Chinese Cinema.* Lanham, MD: Rowman and Littlefield, 2007.

Yang, Daqing. "The Challenges of the Nanjing Massacre: Reflections on Historical Inquiry." In Joshua A. Fogel, ed., *The Nanjing Massacre in History and Historiography*. Berkeley and Los Angeles: University of California Press, 2000.

Yü, Chün-fang. "Guanyin: The Chinese Transformation of Avalokitesvara." In Marsha Weidner, ed., *Latter Days of the Law: Images of Chinese Buddhism, 850–1850*, 150–181. Lawrence and Honolulu: University of Kansas Spencer Museum of Art and University of Hawaii Press, 1994.

Zeitlin, Judith. *The Phantom Heroine: Ghosts and Gender in Seventeenth-Century Chinese Literature*. Honolulu: University of Hawai'i Press, 2007.

——. *Historian of the Strange: Pu Songling and the Chinese Classical Tale*. Stanford: Stanford University Press, 1993.

Zhang, Yingjin. *Screening China: Critical Interventions, Cinematic Reconfigurations, and the Transnational Imaginary in Contemporary Chinese Cinema*. Ann Arbor: Center for Chinese Studies, University of Michigan, 2002.

Zhang Zhen, ed. *The Urban Generation: Chinese Cinema and Society at the Turn of the Twenty-first Century*. Durham: Duke University Press, 2007.

Zhu Qi, ed. *1990 nian yilai de Zhongguo xianfeng sheying, Chinese Avant-garde Photography Since 1990*. Changsha: Hunan meishu chubanshe, 2004.

Zimbardo, Philip. *The Lucifer Effect: Understanding How Good People Turn Evil*. New York: Random House, 2007.

Zito, Angela, and Tani E. Barlow. *Body, Subject, and Power in China*. Chicago: University of Chicago Press, 1994.

List of Illustrations

DVD Film Clips

In the Heat of the Sun

Scene 1. In the Classroom
Preceded by the narrator's comment, "The older kids were in the villages or army and the town belonged to us," this classroom scene delivers a view of authority under duress during the Cultural Revolution. But the goings-on also question whether we can, or should, believe our own eyes.

Scene 2. The Girl-in-Red
As Ma Xiaojun steals into an apartment, his heart is stolen by a lovely photograph. But does the photograph really exist?

Scene 3. An Assault on Memory
Rejection and resentment boil over, and Ma Xiaojun attacks his rival for Mi Lan's affections. Or does he?

Scene 4. Epilogue in Black-and-White
As the credits roll, the audience may stand up to walk out. But as the photography shifts from color to black-and-white and the film's youthful characters are now briefly seen all grown up, the scene offers subtle clues to the purpose of this film.

Devils on the Doorstep

Scene 1. "Wo" / "Me"
The film's main character, Ma Dasan, and his illicit lover, the widow Yu'er, are interrupted in the middle of night. The plot is set in motion by a peculiar delivery from an anonymous, gun-wielding messenger.

Scene 2. Interrogation
The antagonists face off, with contrary purposes and language deficits that lead to uncertainty about who is questioning whom and just what the answers mean.

Scene 3. The Prisoners Returned
The "peculiar delivery" from scene one — a captured Japanese soldier and his Chinese translator — is delivered back to Japanese custody. But just as a solution to the villagers' predicament is found and prospects seem to be looking up, reality sets in and the future becomes more threatening than ever. Animal behavior both triggers the turn of events and symbolizes the situation.

Scene 4. Justice
Having survived the Japanese occupation, Ma Dasan is sentenced by his fellow Chinese to die at the hands of the Japanese, and eventually by the same Japanese soldier, peculiarly delivered, whom he managed to save. Once again, the relation between man and beast is explored.

Tang Center Lecture Series

2003   Wen C. Fong
Three Lectures on Chinese Art History

2007   Anne de Coursey Clapp
Commemorative Landscape Painting in China
Publication forthcoming

2007   Jerome Silbergeld
Body Talk, in Two Chinese Films by Director Jiang Wen
Published in 2008 as *Body in Question: Image and Illusion in Two Chinese Films by Director Jiang Wen*